# RELEA~~~ ...~
# FROZEN ASSETS

A look at the role of women in the church

## Rachel Hickson
### with Helen Azer

Produced by Heartcry for Change
www.heartcryforchange.com

# Dedication

I dedicate this book to **Gordon**, my incredible husband, who has been my greatest cheerleader and constantly inspired and challenged me to speak, lead and pioneer new things. He is an amazing man!

Rachel Hickson

# Contents

# Acknowledgements

This part of the book is impossible to write!

How can you express your gratitude to each person who deserves it?

I am sure I will forget someone – so thank you!

But I do want to thank my husband, **Gordon**, to whom I have dedicated my portion of this book. He has often taken the heat for having a wife who is a woman leader and he has never complained. You are such a great encourager!

I want to thank **Helen Azer**, my co-author, who has written and researched considerable sections of this book for me. She is an incredible person, theologically trained, who loves reading complicated texts, and without her this book would have been much more difficult.

I also want to thank an army of volunteers who have read the manuscript, advised me on the theology and content, helped correct my grammar and given me hope.

Thank you for all your reading time!

Finally thank *you* for buying this book.

I hope that it will be more than just another book but that it will inspire you to see God release His women into their rightful role in these days.

So now ENJOY and be ready to change!

# Foreword

Perhaps it would be good for you to hear from me, as Rachel's husband, before you dive into a personal story and the complex theology and reasoning contained in this book! My background was ten years as an Army Officer, five years as a Business Director with my own company, five years as Crusade Director in Africa and Asia for Christ for all Nations, followed by twenty years of pastoring and directing missions. Obviously I am biased, but let me share with you some of the journey that I have had in moving from a very male chauvinist perspective (all male education and then ten years with soldiers!) to a position of now delighting in releasing and recognizing one of the most anointed women leaders that I know.

My journey began in 1989, after four years of organizing Reinhard Bonnke's campaigns. We arrived in Kuala Lumpur to organize an evangelistic campaign in the National Stadium. Till that moment, Rachel had just followed me as a wife and mother of two small children, and she had never ministered. Due to the sensitivity of working in an Islamic nation, I took time out, away from home, to pray for wisdom about whether to cancel our campaign plans. God spoke a verse clearly to me from Joel 3 to go ahead. I was then amazed on returning to KL to hear that Rachel had had an encounter with God the same night and He had given her the same verse...and told her to begin to preach in the churches to mobilize prayer for the campaign.

A short while after this, I called together many of the pastors and leaders of KL to talk about our dreams for the campaign. As I was about to start, my "little Rachel" signaled to me from the front row and said that she felt that God had given her a word for that evening. From my rather chauvinist perspective, I assumed that perhaps she had a little word of encouragement or a picture she wanted to share, so I gave her the microphone. What happened next was destined to change my life! My "little Rachel" walked up onto the platform and I watched as a mantle of anointing fell on her: she preached without notes for about one hour, with such confidence and authority that every one of us knew that God had just spoken to us! One of the Campaign committee, who had been a Member of Parliament, sat spell bound as he watched angels above Rachel's head blowing trumpets!

"Who is this lady?!", I thought. I couldn't recognize her as she drew a line across the platform with her foot, and shouted out: "You've come this far, Devil, but no further...Back off!" As she finished, there was such an anointing in the building and people who tried to approach her were touched by the Spirit. Then suddenly, after a while, it lifted and my "little Rachel" emerged: that was the first time I became aware that I had to respect both the "little Rachel", to whom I was married, and the "ministry Rachel" who suddenly appeared as the anointing of the Spirit fell on her. Thus began my journey of discovering that, under the anointing, "in Christ" there is neither male nor female. I should mention that Rachel then single-handedly spent the next few months mobilizing a massive army of prayer warriors, and this was the primary reason for one of the most miraculous breakthroughs we had ever seen in our time of organizing evangelistic campaigns.

Soon after this campaign we left Christ for All Nations (CfaN) and returned to the UK for me to take up a position as Senior Pastor over four churches which related to one of the apostolic streams of ministry that could not accept the role of women in ministry. Both of us were very compliant, and so I led the churches with an all-male eldership and, sadly, never for a moment questioned what this would mean for Rachel and myself...let alone all the other wives and women called to lead or minister. It soon became apparent to all of us elders that many times when we made a decision in the Eldership, each husband would go home and share the decision with his wife, only to return a week later to confess that perhaps there was a totally different perspective we needed to take into account! We all knew why each of us had changed our minds! It took us a while before we finally accepted that we were just playing religious games and we really needed to accept that God designed both Church and family to be led by men and women in harmony. Right government and peace flowed together from this place, and it brought us into a time of peace as the leaders in the Church.

It was during these early years back in the UK that I witnessed the devastating effect that this all-male leadership was having on Rachel. My "ministry Rachel" had been put back in a cage and this damaged my "little Rachel": she was sick all the time and lived with a constant sense of being second class and unable to fulfil the ministry call on her life. It strained our intimacy and communication, having spent the last years with CfaN flying high as two eagles, working closely together in leading the campaign in Malaysia. It was only after three years of living under this chauvinist religious atmosphere that something broke in Rachel and from deep within she cried, "I've got to be me! I'm born to preach and I cannot deny what God has called me to do."

From this moment, the ministry of Heartcry was born, with Rachel initially just ministering to women in women's conferences all over the country. This was destined to change - not through anything Rachel initiated, but through God's intervention. It just happened that her women's conference was co-located with the Vineyard Leaders' Conference. Quite a number of the men from the other conference began to sit at the back of her meetings. They insisted that men should be allowed into her conferences because they loved her preaching, and God was doing some amazing things! This triggered the birth of the "Shoulder to Shoulder" conferences for both men and women, but the conferences were led by Rachel and the Heartcry women! I should say that I often ministered alongside Rachel at these conferences but everyone knew where the leadership came from!

To conclude, let me just say that I feel immensely proud every time I watch my "ministry Rachel" flying high and touching nation after nation. I was deeply touched a few years ago to open a national Christian newspaper in Norway, only to find a photo of my Rachel in the centre page: over the top of the picture was the headline "A Spiritual Mother for Norway?". It was at that time that I just stood back amazed at how God had anointed Rachel to be a spiritual mother to so many. Who was I to argue with the wisdom of the Almighty! For me it is the greatest honour to be known in many places around the world as..."Rachel's husband!"

Gordon Hickson

# Introduction and comment

I have a confession to make – I am a coward. Many of those who know me think of me as a confident, secure woman who never panics. Wrong! I know writing a book about this topic is like playing with fire and I do not want to get burnt – hence the coward!

However, I also know so many of you have asked me genuine questions over the years and it is time to try to unpack the answers and make them clear for us. I am so grateful to Helen who has partnered with me in writing this book. Her input, especially into some of the difficult texts on the theology of women, has been invaluable. Thank you.

But, just in case this sentiment does not come through clearly in the book, I want to say at the beginning that I have a great respect and admiration for men in leadership. I have learnt so much even from those men who would never let me speak in their pulpits and probably would believe I am deceived, a "jezebel", or worse! I have read a wide range of authors in my study of scripture and have appreciated the incredible contributions of many conservative theologians who would not agree with my position of leadership. But I love their insight into so many other areas of theology. In this book we have concentrated on the role of women but in no way would I want to disregard the amazing men who have helped me in my journey. My heart is always to have men and women working together with a mutual respect for each other's gift.

I also want to say that I am not a feminist, and I find the strong campaigning position "that women MUST be given a place" disturbing. I believe that we should serve each other with our gifts and abilities and always help each other excel. I do not believe that women should be given a place for equality's sake and to keep the peace. I believe that we should all seek to have the right person in the right place at the right time and if this is a woman then so be it! I have always been cautious of doing something "to prove a woman can do it" and have tried to avoid these play offs.

Finally, I have an amazing husband and he has released me to fly into all my areas of gifting. He has always held me on an open hand and encouraged me. This has given me great freedom. I know he has paid the price of misunderstanding at times and been accused of being a "weak" man as he could not keep his wife in her place. But I am so grateful that he still let me be me. He is my hero!

So please hear my heart as you read this book – I do not want to stir trouble but just express our sincere belief that this is the time for women to be released into their full potential and, as we fly free, remember we do respect and need the men in our lives too!

Rachel Hickson

# 1 Hearing the cry for women to arise

Yet again I found myself being invited to speak at a women's conference and, if I am honest, I was not overjoyed. I preferred to speak to congregations of men and women together and found these "girls only" meetings difficult. But my hesitancy to speak at women only events was irritated by this invitation and I found myself asking God if I should go, even though it was not my personal choice. As I prayed, I was surprised to hear God speak to me so clearly: "Rachel, I am asking you to go and take my word and speak to these women with encouragement – it is TIME to release my frozen assets and I want to use you as a mouth piece!" I realized God was asking me to bring a word of freedom and deliverance to many women. It was time to break the chains of captivity in their minds and speak the word – "LET MY WOMEN GO!" Since this encounter I have given much of my time to women and counted it a joy every time I watch them grasp the message of freedom. Being with girls at women's conferences as they meet together to discover God is now one of my favourite adventures all around the world. God loves celebrating with His girls as they step into their freedom.

## A look at my story

I myself have had to walk this journey of freedom. For years I had felt guilty that my leadership skills were placed in a female body and wished I had been born a man so that these gifts would be celebrated rather than criticised by some leaders in the church. I wanted to be able to function to the full extent of my capacity without being labelled "a powerful woman" which, I had learnt, was not a compliment but usually meant I was a threat or rebellious. I longed for the freedom to be truly myself as a woman leader. Over the years I have had to learn to take the criticism without being defensive and speak boldly without being overwhelmed by fear. Like everyone else I have had to learn to fulfil my purpose and calling without compromise or intimidation controlling me, and this has been a road of tough choices that does not necessarily make you popular. However, as I have learnt to obey, lead and speak and have loved the people, I have found that God has opened amazing doors of opportunity and friendship. I have been blessed and opposed, I have been loved and accused, but overall I have been overwhelmed by the goodness of God. It is such a privilege to serve God, men, women and children and carry His message of hope and watch lives transformed. I love it!

As I began to meet God's precious girls of all ages, cultures and backgrounds, I discovered some amazing women of service, gifting and vision who were hesitant to function in the church. Many of them had already been recognized as exceptional leaders throughout their school and college days: they had been the head of school or the student college representative and then had been rapidly promoted as managers in their places of work. However, many of them felt insecure concerning their role in their church environment. Are women allowed to excel as gifted leaders in the church? Should women hide their leadership skills or express their vision and gifts? Can you only be a woman leader if you are married to a church leader? This gender struggle of our roles and function has resulted in some women becoming fatigued with church politics and so choosing to keep their personal faith vibrant with God but deliberately choosing to take a less prominent role in their local church. Others had continued to try to serve their local church with their full potential but encountered many challenges and had become hurt and discouraged, while still others confessed that they had never let anyone in the church know that they were talented, gifted people. They had just made the decision to separate their training and responsibilities in the work place from their church life. They were leaders on Monday to Friday at work and then hid behind the "just a mum" label at church. However, this is an uncomfortable compromise as these leaders are gifted and love to serve and to be fully present in the moment. If their giftedness is seen as a challenge to men – or worse, a rebellious spirit – eventually the fire of their passion dies and they feel crushed as individuals. The issue of a woman's function in the church is much more far reaching and complex than whether we believe that women should speak. We must also ask whether we believe that some women are born as leaders. For if we believe some women are born to lead then we must surely also allow them to teach, train and equip the next generation of men and women.

*Prophetic words concerning women in leadership*

While God has been challenging some women in a personal way to take their place of leadership, God has also been speaking prophetically through various men and women about the role of women at this time in history. There is a famous prophetic word given by an abbess challenging women to pray and saying that Britain would be saved by praying women. The prophecy was brought by Mother Barbara (Abbess of the Convent of the Garden of Gethsemane in Jerusalem) from Russia in 1911. The prophecy was given by one of the monks there who was praying for her father in a monastery north of Moscow. She had gone there to ask them to pray for her father who was in danger. As a result, she believes they were able to leave Russia. She went to Jerusalem where she has lived ever since. (I believe she died a few years ago.) When the monks were praying for her father, one of them had prophesied and she had written it all down. She translated the prophecy from Russian and this is part of it:

"An evil will shortly overtake Russia and wherever this evil comes, rivers of blood will flow. It is not the Russian soul, but an imposition on the Russian soul. It is not an ideology, or a philosophy, but a spirit from hell. In the last days Germany will be divided in two. France will just be nothing. Italy will be judged by natural disasters. Britain will lose her empire and all her colonies and will come to almost total ruin, **but will be saved by praying women.** America will feed the world, but will finally collapse... Finally Russia will be free and from her, believers will go forth and turn many from the nations to God...." The old monk then said to her: "You will live to see Russia free, but you will not live to see the Antichrist." This is a prophetic challenge to women to find their authority in the place of prayer.

Later in the 20th century others wrote and spoke about the place of women in leadership. Jim Goll and other prophets have been saying over and over that this decade is the "season of the women." James Goll, a father in the Body of Christ from the USA, simply gave a strategic word: "Let the Women Speak!". The Lord had said to him recently: "There is great strength in motherhood and nurturing. Women's characteristics are sometimes overlooked and not seen as a quality of strength, but it's truly the opposite. The definition of nurture is: to feed and protect, to support and encourage, to bring up, to train, to educate." Goll continues to say that these characteristics are what everyone on the face of this earth needs to be able to grow and develop. He strongly believes that God is raising His qualities in women to be displayed at this time. Why? Because the world simply needs to know more of these attributes. Whether you are a physical or spiritual mother or both, or still in your youth, your qualities are greatly needed and deeply valued by God, states Goll. He declares it is time for a season of nurture and mothering in the nations and the women need to arise!

## Pastors and leaders speak out about women

**Ed Silvoso,** from Argentina, also writes about women being a strategic part of the end time harvest in his book called *Women: God's Secret Weapon*. Surprisingly, many of these voices are coming from nations where women have been despised and abused. Silvoso's book is "a potent teaching from a respected leader on the potential of women in ministry. Ed Silvoso takes a fresh look at the Fall in Genesis, specifically how it relates to women's ultimate role in defeating Satan. He contends that Satan fears women whose seed will deliver the final fatal blow to his kingdom. Silvoso unfolds practical steps that need to occur for women to be restored to their God-given positions of effective ministry and presents powerful examples of what happens when women are 'twice refined' then released into ministry. This book emboldens women to step beyond stereotypical roles and find healing from long-term emotional hurts. It also establishes biblically and lays out principles which will enable men to have a strategy and confidence that they can walk side by side with women, helping them to be restored and refined. Ed Silvoso then challenges women to be released from all captivity and to participate in the end time harvest. He believes that it is time for a great host of women to arise with Good News and carry the message of evangelism into our communities.[1]"

There are other voices from many cultural backgrounds and nations also expressing their conviction that this is the time when women should be released to find their function and role in the church. These leaders are often from

---

[1] Quote from official book description, Regal Books, 2001

cultures where women would naturally be silenced and suppressed but the church leaders here have given them a voice. **David Yonggi Cho, senior pastor of the 700,000-member Yoido Full Gospel Church in Seoul,** has said: "For 5,000 years in Korea, women had no voice at all. They were only considered necessary to cater for the needs of men. But then Christianity came and set women free. Especially in the church, women are free. In ministry, they are equal to men. They are licensed; they are ordained. They become deacons and elders, and they become cell leaders". Pastor Cho suggests that if pastors will train women and delegate ministry to them, they will become tremendous messengers for the Lord. Although some argue that women should be silent in church, Cho argues further that once women are called into ministry, they no longer belong to the category of women, they are now messengers of the Lord. They now function because of their spiritual calling, not because of their gender!

**Chuck Pierce** also examines the role of women and their place in leadership in chapter nine of his book, *The Future War of the Church*. He concludes that God is renewing and restoring the apostolic gifting in the Body of Christ and He is raising up leadership for the future. He states that God is releasing an anointing for spiritual breakthrough against the kingdom of darkness from region to region at this time. This is a season when our Lord's apostolic order and authority are being established in a new, fresh dimension. Part of God's order for this hour is the establishment of godly women with an authority, says Chuck Pierce, and he believes that as a result a greater sphere of influence will then revolutionize societies throughout the earth.

Many prophets are declaring that there will be a great move of the Holy Spirit amongst and upon women. As the Spirit moves I also believe we will see many women being called to preach, teach and evangelize cities and nations just as these prophetic men have described. Many women will find themselves released and liberated to go forth and proclaim in their communities and the nations: "The kingdom of our Lord is at hand!" But is the church ready to work shoulder to shoulder with vibrant women as leaders?

# 2 Why the "woman issue" again?!

Very often this is the response of church leaders when asked about the subject of the role of women, women in leadership, and what they believe concerning the "difficult scriptures" in the Bible which appear to restrict the function of women in the Church. Most of these leaders are men who have settled this theological issue in their minds many years ago and so they do not see it as a relevant point for discussion any longer. Since this issue does not directly affect their function as men, they are usually unaware of the spiritual repercussions which continue to affect women. They express their openness to fully endorse women as part of their leadership teams and so do not see the need to rake over old ground again. Having made this decision, many leaders are completely unaware that, although they may have clarified their personal theological journey in this area concerning women in leadership, many in their congregations are still untaught and confused.

But while there is a whole generation of leaders in church today who feel they have "been there and done that" and settled the matter in their minds years ago, still the voice of many others in the conservative evangelical wing of the Church, as well as the Roman Catholic and Orthodox traditions, insists that women in leadership is unbiblical.

Of those who are prepared to work alongside women in ministry and affirm their role in leadership, some would still restrict their function, for example stopping short of appointing female elders, or, at least in practice, only ever appointing married couples to positions of more senior or more prominent leadership. This is usually connected with the theology of male headship authority, hierarchical models of leadership and, in some instances, a hesitation about appointing single women who do not have a husband as their covering. This means that in churches where women are functioning freely, the model is often that of a husband and wife team. There are rarely examples or role models of single women teachers (such as a female "John Stott"). This also raises pastoral questions about the role of a woman leader if her husband should die before her: would she, for example, be allowed to continue in her leadership of the church or ministry?

A further consideration is that many who are exploring faith in our churches have come from un-churched backgrounds and, when asked, are under the misconception that the Bible is anti-women and that Christianity is misogynistic just like all other major world religions. The lack of teaching on this issue as part of our regular discipleship programmes is frequently a stumbling block to the gospel and a cause of offence, especially to the younger generation of men and women.

The younger generation, who are products of a postmodern worldview, have been taught by culture that "anything goes", and have a justice protocol of "equal rights" for everyone. In their world your gender has no limitations on your function; you can be whatever you want to be as long as you train and have the skill set to accomplish it. However, some of these new believers are asking questions on behalf of themselves or their sisters, wives and daughters. They want to know if this liberation of women in society has been a good thing or if it is just another "sign of the times" which the Church should resist. Is there such a thing as "biblical feminism" i.e. does the Bible teach gender equality or is this just a product of political correctness? Their honest questioning should be taken seriously as it stems from a genuine desire to honour God in a society where Christianity is under increasing attack.

Many Christians have seen anointed women function as teachers, preachers and leaders and so cannot understand why some within the Church would not accept that God calls and anoints women as well as men. In the absence of a commitment to teach what the Bible really says about women, many young men and women feel confused and unsure about how they should understand the difficult scripture passages which appear to prohibit women from teaching and restrict their role in ministry and leadership.

In Genesis we are told that one of the most fundamental areas of spiritual warfare would be between "woman-kind" and Satan, and between the sexes. We need to be aware that this spiritual battle still rages and help men and women combat it through the application of the Word of God. Just because we may feel as leaders we have "settled this issue in our minds", we must not neglect our duty to teach and inform the next generation on this vitally important issue.

Statistics suggest that on average over 70% of the church congregations are women. As leaders we would consider it our responsibility to teach them about their identity, money and character issues so why do we hesitate to teach them about their role as women in the church? If the enemy can paralyze 70% of the Church through ignorance or poor theology, then we should not be surprised if the Church sometimes appears confused or powerless. However, the "women's issue" is not just an issue for women; it also affects how men and women relate and function together in a church and ultimately influences the cohesion and strength of the church family. The history of revivals in nations such as China and Korea shows that, in so many cases, it was not until women were fully mobilized and released that the Church began to grow significantly. In these days, the same testimony from the Middle East suggests that history is repeating itself and the same pattern is emerging. As women find their leadership role so the growth of the church and evangelism are strengthened.

If the witness of revival history and the sense from prophetic voices around the world (both male and female!) is that now is the time for God's "frozen assets" to be released, can we afford not to consider this subject afresh?

## Women and the Gay issue?!

This slogan, "the Women's and the Gay Issue", has been increasingly used in the media and then the church over the last years until these two issues have become intrinsically linked in our minds. Both these issues have been presented together as campaigns for justice on the one hand, or a cause for concern about error and deception on the other. This unfortunate linking of the objections to women in leadership with concerns about the liberal stance towards homosexuality has caused confusion and further caution for many in the church. This issue has become further exacerbated by the discussions in the General Synod of the Church of England. Media reports of the Synod's business have continued to present the headlines as the Church debating "the Women's and the Gay Issue". This, in turn, has led to a number of church leaders reconsidering their position on women in ministry, fearing that a permissive attitude towards women could be misinterpreted by their congregation as also having a liberal stance on homosexuality, or, worse, that this stance could lead their church into error.

## How do they arrive at this conclusion?

Their argument runs that if the Bible states in 1 Timothy 2:12 "*I do not permit a woman to teach or to have authority over a man*" and yet we do not read this literally but seek to contextualize these words in the culture of the day, then what would prevent the same attitude being applied to Leviticus 18:22 "*'Do not have sexual relations with a man as one does with a woman; that is detestable.*" Can we justify reading some biblical commands literally and apply them universally and for all time, while contextualizing others?

## Problems with this line of reasoning

a) The most fundamental failure in the argument above is in the misunderstanding of the application of the law of God in the Bible. Scholars generally agree that there are three types of law: moral, ceremonial and civil (judicial). Of these, God's moral law never changes in Scripture. It is consistent throughout and eternally applicable. This law would cover our understanding of character issues, truth and integrity, murder and our respect for life, marriage and the principles that govern sexual conduct, and many other areas. Ceremonial law, on the other hand, which was concerned with the sacrificial system, the atonement for sin and laws regulating worship, does change. Jesus comes to fulfil much of this law by becoming the sacrificial lamb. Likewise, circumcision is replaced with the circumcision of the heart and so on. Civil law is that which is applicable in the society and culture of the day. This covers much of the context of Paul's epistles which necessitate him "laying down the (civil) law" for specific situations in order to address matters arising in local practice such as the treatment of slaves, the wearing of head coverings and the customs surrounding the length of men's and women's hair. While authoritative for the recipient of Paul's letters, these regulations never claim to be universal nor have the weight of divine, moral edicts. Instead, their authority lies in the principle or spirit, rather than the letter, of the law.

b) Issues surrounding worship in the early church are specific to the context and governed by the civil practices and customs of the day. In many instances they are also concessions to the customs of the day with Paul acknowledging that in Christ there is absolute freedom and equality for both genders, but for the sake of the culture and of the gospel spreading unhindered, women should choose to restrict their own actions voluntarily in submission to "civil law".

c) However, homosexuality falls into the category of moral law. Nowhere in the Bible is the act of homosexuality described as anything other than a sin that is offensive to God. There is never a sense in the New Testament that this is an attitude dictated by a concession to culture. Quite to the contrary, Paul often states the case against the act of homosexuality in spite of the far more permissive societal and cultic sexual practices of his day.

The problem then with linking our biblical interpretation of these passages on sexual conduct with those about women is that there are very distinctive biblical categories of law which require a completely different hermeneutical approach. We cannot equate God's attitude to the act of homosexuality with His attitude towards the gender of a woman. Nowhere in the Bible does it say that being female is an abomination, or that the act of a woman speaking or teaching is detestable. So, as it is not our remit to discuss a biblical theology of sex and sexuality in this book, we will confine our comments to simply emphasizing that we believe the "woman's issue" deserves consideration in its own right. We also believe that it is perfectly possible to support women as they function in their leadership roles without the "danger" of becoming a liberal theologian!

# 3 Walking with God's girls through the Bible

## *Steps on my journey to freedom*

It was Easter Sunday 1993 and I was lying in hospital. I had a lump in my breast, a suspected kidney stone and had been bleeding for 19 days from my uterus. Every area of my feminine privacy felt like it had been invaded by the various medical tests and I felt sorry for myself and discouraged. As I lay in bed complaining to God I felt Him speak to me so clearly: "Rachel, what would satisfy you? What life do you want?" In that moment I began to remember my days in Malaysia.

Gordon and I had the privilege of working with Reinhard Bonnke and the Christ for all Nations team and in 1998 we were sent to Malaysia. Gordon was the Crusade Director and I was a mum with two small children who travelled with him. However, when we arrived in Kuala Lumpur we encountered many difficulties as we began to plan and I found myself in a season of deep intercession for breakthrough in this nation. We had planned many prayer events across the city and were waiting for the arrival of Suzette Hattingh who was to come and minister. However, at the last moment her visa was refused and she was not able to come. In desperation Gordon turned to me and asked me to help. "Rachel, you could do this; would you teach on prayer at the early morning prayer meetings?" Suddenly I found myself launched into speaking. I was terrified and questioned whether I should even do this, but I knew Gordon needed my help. To my surprise I discovered I loved to teach. I loved to study the Bible. I loved watching people grasp the principles and fall in love with Jesus. I was satisfied! This was wonderful!

Tears flowed down my face in the open ward as I remembered these moments. I knew God was speaking to me and deep inside I found myself crying out: "God, I want to speak! God, I want to be free – I want to be the real me!!" Gordon and I had returned to the UK in 1990 and were part of a leadership structure that did not release women to speak. This had been explained to us when we returned home and I had accepted it. However, as we had begun to function in these new roles I felt bereft. Gordon was leading with the men and I was at home with the growing kids, but feeling unfulfilled. Gordon and I had partnered so closely together on the mission field and now I was alone at home. I was not angry about this turn of events and considered it to be right and what God wanted, yet I felt so confused by my feeling of constraint and dissatisfaction. I dared not express any of these emotions publicly for fear of being seen as "rebellious" or a "jezebel" and I did not want to cause Gordon any further stress. So, I decided, I just needed to cope and sort myself out. But here in this hospital bed I realised I was not coping on the inside. Deep within the core of my being was a cry – "Please let me GO! I just want to be me!"

Still with the tears on my face I noticed Gordon had arrived and it was visiting time. Then I noticed Gordon no longer had the worried look that had greeted me these last days but a new glow of confidence. Suddenly he took my hand and looked me straight in the eyes and said clearly: "Rachel, I have it – I have the answer – I know why you are sick and I am so sorry. Please forgive me!" I was not sure what had happened but I knew Gordon had had an encounter. He then told me about a dream he had had that night. He said he had fallen asleep worried and praying for me. (Gordon is so tender and he hated seeing me in pain and sick.) As he fell asleep God spoke to him in a dream. He saw a picture of an eagle, a majestic beautiful bird, but it was trapped in a budgerigar cage. The eagle looked sick and its wings were damaged. As he looked at this bird God spoke to him and said: "Eagles in cages become sick birds – they must be allowed to fly!" Instantly he knew this was why I was sick. He had watched me fly in Malaysia as I had taught and partnered alongside him in the ministry but now I was caged by restrictions and I was sick!

With tears now flowing down his face he looked at me with deep sincerity and asked for my forgiveness. But there was little to forgive, for we had both agreed together that it was right for me to sit back and not teach; we had thought it was the right advice even though deep down we had felt confused. Then Gordon said to me: "Rachel, I am opening the door to the cage. Rachel, we will do whatever we need to do to bring this change but please be free. I want to have my Rachel back – please be you. Just FLY!" In that moment I realised that God had heard my cry before I had even expressed it and had given Gordon the key to unlock my cage. I was free. This eagle had found her wings! However, it does not mean that life was easy from now on. We encountered criticism and misunderstanding but Gordon has walked with me through every step, but more of my story later.

## The function and role of women in the Bible and early church

I have told you some of my personal journey into the ministry but let us now take a walk through the Bible and examine the lives of some amazing women, look at their responsibilities and the lessons they learnt. The Bible is such a real book full of stories about normal life. So let us go on this journey of discovery with the female heroes of our faith.

## Women were in Paul's apostolic team
*Romans 16: 1-11*

### Phoebe

**Romans 16: 1-2**
*I commend to you our sister Phoebe, a deacon of the church in Cenchreae. 2 I ask you to receive her in the Lord in a way worthy of his people and to give her any help she may need from you, for she has been the benefactor of many people, including me.*

Paul commended this woman to the church and asked them to receive her as in the Lord. He refers to her as *diakonon*, the Greek word for Deacon, which translated as servant here and carried the sense of one sent to work with the overseers and elders.

It would be more accurate to place her alongside Stephen and Philip as the same word *diakonon* was used to describe them. Paul's introduction of her to the church in Rome was his way of establishing her honour and authority on her arrival. She was sent by Paul to help in the establishment of the church, specifically in relation to evangelism and church planting. Remember the deacons were known for their powerful miracles and work.

Young's Literal Translation translates verse two as follows: *...that ye may receive her in the Lord, as doth become saints, and may assist her in whatever matter she may have need of you -- for she also **became a leader of many, and of myself**.*

The word translated leader here is the Greek word "*protostates*" which meant one who is prominent, has "rule" or leadership. In the Roman understanding it would be one who stood in the front rank such as a chief, champion or leader. It is the same word used in 1 Timothy 5:17 where it says that elders who rule (*epostatis*) well are worthy of double honour.

### Priscilla and Aquila

**Romans 16: 3**
*Greet Priscilla and Aquila, my co-workers in Christ Jesus.*

Priscilla is mentioned alongside her husband and is honoured as Paul's co-worker. The passage suggests that this was an apostolic couple whom Paul related to well and commended for the church which met in their home. At times Priscilla is mentioned ahead of her husband and at other times Aquila is first. There seems to be no differentiation between them and both are honoured for their leadership by Paul.

## Junia

**Romans 16: 7**
*Greet Andronicus and Junia, my fellow Jews who have been in prison with me. They are outstanding among the apostles, and they were in Christ before I was.*

The meaning of this verse is unambiguous: Paul is commending two people as outstanding apostles. But this verse has created quite a controversy because of the mention of Junia, a recognized name for a woman in Paul's day. Could Paul really have meant to include a woman among the list of apostles in the early church? So scandalized were some church theologians and translators of the Bible that the earliest documents which clearly had the female name were amended to Junias, the male version of the name! It would be like amending Pauline to Paul. Although the female root of the Greek is used, many theologians have considered it an error so they translate it JUNIAS rather than retain the female JUNIA, and this male form was then used as a basis for the Latin translation of the Bible.

Attempts to change her name in the manuscripts of the Bible probably did not occur until the 13th century according to scholars. The theologians argued it must be an error, NOT because the text was confusing, as the text is clear, but because of their position that a woman could not be an apostle. They read into the text from the standpoint of their prejudice rather than allow the text to challenge and correct their theology.[2]

---

[2] For a fuller examination of this read Epp, Eldon Jay, *Junia: The First Woman Apostle*, Fortress Press 2005

**Mary, Tryphena, Tryphosa, Mother of Rufus, Sister of Nereus, Julia**

These women are listed as fellow workers, fellow prisoners for the Gospel. They are all commended by Paul.

## God includes rather than excludes

I was standing in front of a large Sunday congregation, having just been introduced as the speaker for that service, when I noticed that many of the people looked confused and even alarmed. As I wondered about the cause of this strange reaction, the pastor who had introduced me suddenly interrupted me and asked if he could have the microphone back as he needed to make a further announcement. The reaction I had noticed now made sense! The pastor explained to his people that although he had taught in the past that he did not believe a woman should teach on a Sunday morning God had spoken to him to allow me to speak to the church. He then said: "I do not see Rachel as a 'woman' but as a servant of God. Please will you receive her as I believe she will bring us a word from God." Some people have been offended by this story wondering why the pastor denied my femininity. But I saw this introduction as a compliment. He was asking his people to look beyond the gender issue. He was saying, when I look at Rachel, I do not see a woman first but I can look beyond her gender and see someone who carries Jesus. WOW – this blessed me!

I believe that God does not exclude people from ministry on the basis of their gender. Although we are of a definite gender – male or female – God does not differentiate concerning our spiritual life or anointing on the basis of our gender any more than He would on the basis of our race or cultural background.

**Galatians 3:27-28**
*For all of you who were baptized into Christ have clothed yourselves with Christ.* ***28*** *There is neither Jew nor Greek, slave nor free, **male nor female**, for you are all one in Christ Jesus.*

There are no racial, social or gender barriers in our spiritual life – all are equal. So let us celebrate who we are and carry Jesus like these amazing women we will read about.

## Women through the Bible

### a) Miriam

She was the sister of Moses and Aaron and considered a leader in ancient Israel.

**Micah 6:4**
*I brought you up out of Egypt and redeemed you from the land of slavery. I sent Moses to lead you, also Aaron and Miriam.*

God sent Moses, Aaron and Miriam "to LEAD you". She represented God's authority to the people in the same way that Moses did. She was also a prophetess who led congregational worship.

**Exodus 15:20**
*Then Miriam the prophet, Aaron's sister, took a timbrel in her hand, and all the women followed her, with timbrels and dancing.*

## b) Deborah

She was among the judges of Israel.

**Judges 4: 4**
*Now Deborah, a prophet, the wife of Lappidoth, was leading Israel at that time.*

**Judges 4:6-8**
*She sent for Barak son of Abinoam from Kedesh in Naphtali and said to him, "The Lord, the God of Israel, commands you: 'Go, take with you ten thousand men of Naphtali and Zebulun and lead them up to Mount Tabor. 7 I will lead Sisera, the commander of Jabin's army, with his chariots and his troops to the Kishon River and give him into your hands.'" 8 Barak said to her, "If you go with me, I will go; but if you don't go with me, I won't go."*

**Judges 5:31**
*"So may all your enemies perish, Lord! But may all who love you be like the sun when it rises in its strength." Then the land had peace forty years.*

Deborah held the position of a prophet as did Samuel. She led the nation in an impressive military victory and for forty years the nation experienced peace. She was strategic in her leadership, carried supernatural wisdom and was known as the Mother of Israel. She was married to Lappidoth, whose name is mentioned once, but he did not seem to share her position of spiritual authority. She worked with the military leader, Barak, in her own right. She was so respected by Barak that he refused to act without her counsel or presence. So Deborah's function did not depend on joint leadership with her husband, she was able to act alone, working with Barak in her leadership. Her "leadership team" consisted of both men and women who led in their own right, with Deborah rising to the position of Judge of Israel.

## c) Huldah

**2 Kings 22:14**

*Hilkiah the priest, Ahikam, Akbor, Shaphan and Asaiah went to speak to the prophet Huldah, who was the wife of Shallum son of Tikvah, the son of Harhas, keeper of the wardrobe. She lived in Jerusalem, in the New Quarter.*

After years of national darkness King Josiah leads the nation back to God in repentance and then asks for a faithful follower of God to be found...they find HULDAH. She was a prophetess who remained faithful to God during Israel's dark time in history.

She lived in Jerusalem with her husband Shallum and King Josiah found her. Her prophetic words to King Josiah came true and the High Priest Hilkiah sought her out so she must have earned the reputation of knowing and hearing from God. She was an influencer and advisor to the King.

## d) Esther

She did not primarily function in ecclesiastical authority but this shows that God places women in significant secular leadership roles within nations too. Like many of us, her instinct was to shrink back, remain silent and not take her place, but in Esther 4:14 we see she was warned not to be intimidated but to speak out on behalf of her nation.

**Esther 4:14**

*For if you remain silent at this time, relief and deliverance for the Jews will arise from another place, but you and your father's family will perish. And who knows but that you have come to royal position for such a time as this?*

Here we see a woman called to a place of influence who has to combat fear and make courageous decisions. Many women have the same potential and gifting today but where are the Mordecais who will encourage these women to speak out and position them with wisdom and advice? Some men would still prefer to keep the women silent and do not seek to encourage them into positions of leadership, or help them find their voice. If women are to find their correct role then we need men correctly positioned too. Men and women must work together!

### e) Philip's Daughters

**Acts 21:9**

*He had four unmarried daughters who prophesied.*

Philip is an evangelist who had four daughters who prophesied. We do not know much about them except that they were influential enough to be mentioned as prophetesses. They were engaged in public speaking and were mentioned alongside Agabus, the male prophet. There is no sense theologically that the Greek word used for prophetess belongs to a second class category of prophets. They are true prophets and their gender is irrelevant to their function. In Acts 15:32 the same word is used to describe Judas and Silas and so, whether prophet or prophetess, they have the same function and anointing.

## f) Lois and Eunice

### 2 Timothy 1:5
*I am reminded of your sincere faith, which first lived in your grandmother Lois and in your mother Eunice and, I am persuaded, now lives in you also.*

Timothy's mother and grandmother were commended by Paul for their teaching, training and development of Timothy. It is ironic that many use 1 Tim 2:12 to show that Paul does not allow a woman to teach, when in 2 Tim 1:5 he commends two women, Lois and Eunice, for the incredible deposit of faith they have taught and passed on to Timothy, his favourite son!

## g) Many others:

**Chloe** – Led the church that Paul was overseeing.

### 1 Corinthians 1:11
*My brothers and sisters, some from Chloe's household have informed me that there are quarrels among you.*

**Nympha** – Had a church that she led in her home.

### Colossians 4:15
*Give my greetings to the brothers and sisters at Laodicea, and to Nympha and the church in her house.*

**Lydia** – seller of purple, a businesswoman and leader who supported Paul.

### Acts 16:40
*After Paul and Silas came out of the prison, they went to Lydia's house, where they met with the brothers and sisters and encouraged them. Then they left.*

**These women held pastoral positions of leading house churches** – but conservative scholars would suggest that they just provided the hospitality but no leadership. The problem with that argument is that no other leader is mentioned and the house church is named after the women.

**Euodia and Syntyche** – women who struggled in the cause of the gospel with Paul. These women were co-labourers in the evangelizing and training of the people. They were more than girls who made the tea!

**Philippians 4:3**

*Yes, and I ask you, my true companion, help these women since they have contended at my side in the cause of the gospel, along with Clement and the rest of my co-workers, whose names are in the book of life.*

# 4 Unpacking those difficult texts about women

So are you ready? When we think about our theology concerning women there are usually several key passages that immediately spring to mind that cause most of the arguments and debates in church life. These are the most controversial verses concerning the role of women and are the root cause of most of our confusion and frustration. So how do we interpret these biblical passages which appear to limit the role of women? In this next section we will look at each problematic passage of scripture and try to discern its true meaning for us in the church today. We will explore the question – should women be allowed to speak? We will tackle these challenging scriptures individually from both the conservative and other points of view and try to reach a considered conclusion from the text. Some texts do appear, on first reading, to be restrictive in regard to the role of women, or even anti-women, but is this conclusion fair? Are there mindsets that we need to change today because of poor theological foundations? Let us look at these passages of scripture together.

But just one more comment before we go on this adventure! We have examined the Greek words in detail, read many books and commentaries and will genuinely try to give a considered and academic summary of our view. However, rather than give the full derivatives of the Greek words in each of these passages in the body of the text, we have summarized our findings in an accessible style for the general reader, but kept the detailed analysis of the Greek for the appendix. If you are interested to explore our conclusions further it is essential that you read the appendix. So happy reading – this was hard work and my brain is still recovering!

## 1) Women Should not Teach - 1 Timothy 2:11-15

**1 Timothy 2:11-15**
*11 A woman should learn in quietness and full submission. 12 I do not permit a woman to teach or to have authority over a man; she must be silent. 13 For Adam was formed first, then Eve. 14 And Adam was not the one deceived; it was the woman who was deceived and became a sinner. 15 But women will be saved through childbearing—if they continue in faith, love and holiness with propriety.*

This is the sole passage that directly examines the subject of gender in leadership within the context of creation order. Conservatives who restrict women's ministry on the basis of their interpretation of this passage would read the scripture as follows:

**1 Timothy 2:11-12**
*(All women) should learn in quietness and full submission (on every matter to all men). I do not permit (any) woman to teach or to have authority over (any) man; she (all women) must be silent."*

On the basis of this interpretation, Paul's first letter to Timothy appears to forbid women to both "teach" and "to have authority over a man" in the church, whilst also calling women to submission and silence (2:11,12).

Conservative scholars have seen the significance given to Adam's prior creation (2:13) as establishing clearly the view that headship is founded on an irrefutable "creation order". George W. Knight, for example, suggests that the text establishes an "order of authority" whereby "the one formed first is to have dominion, the one formed after and from him is to be in subjection". The problem with this reasoning, if taken to its logical conclusion, is that animals would arguably have authority over men because they were formed before men according to the creation accounts! As no scholar is willing to argue this, the justification for male leadership based solely on creation order is hard to sustain. So we must ask what Paul meant by this comment about prior creation.

Paul's reference to Eve being deceived is then interpreted by conservative scholars as legitimating male priority on the basis of an intrinsic moral weakness in woman: Eve, as a "type" of woman, represents woman's greater susceptibility to spiritual influences than that of men. Again, following this line of argument, Adam's undeceived but deliberate disobedience would hardly qualify him for leadership any more than woman if this were the criteria. In fact it might even be possible to argue that a mistaken/ deceived (even gullible!) woman is perhaps preferable to a man who is consciously and deliberately sinful and disobedient. So this again begs the question of whether such a literal reading of Paul's injunction actually gets to the heart of what Paul was saying.

The subsequent instructions that bishops and deacons should be the husband of but one wife (1 Timothy 3:2, 12) are then interpreted as excluding women from these positions in the church. However, some conservative scholars distinguish between women teaching (a doctrinal role) and ministering with a prophetic gift which they consider to be excluded from the definition of authoritative teaching[3]. They would permit a woman to share but not to teach. While this position neatly addresses an awkward apparent contradiction in Paul's argument (prohibiting women from speaking, yet encouraging them to prophesy), it is not a position which can be sustained theologically if we examine the original Greek text.

The Greek usage in this passage suggests a very different translation, namely as follows:

*A wife should learn in quietness and full submission. I am not permitting a wife to teach or to have authority (violently murder, entice, sexually lunge at) over a husband; she must be silent.*

This translation from the Greek gives a very different sense of what Paul is expressing here but also sheds some light on the reasons for his injunction.

**Context:**

Just as in the Corinthian church, there is evidence to suggest that gnostic heresy was widespread in the early Ephesian church and many, especially the women, emphasized spirituality above all. They therefore rejected

---

[3] For a discussion of this view see writings by Knight, George W.

anything, including decency and order as well as their feminine identity, in favour of being a higher spiritual being. Looking at the Ephesian context, Gordon Fee argues that the text is not primarily about church order but about curtailing false teaching, spread by local elders, which was leading people astray (see also 1Timothy 1:3; 4:1; 6:20; Titus 1:11).

So Paul needed to address this and try to stop gnostic heresy spreading from ex-prostitutes who would sexually excite and stimulate audiences, using seductive wiles to persuade and impose their views.

False teaching seems to have been a particular problem among women who were actively spreading it (1Timothy 4:7; 5:11-15; 2 Timothy 3:6), perhaps because they were less educated than men or, alternatively, because the content was particularly attractive to women.

In addition to gnostic influences, scholars point to the presence of the Temple of Artemis in Ephesus. This powerful mother-goddess was served by female priestesses alone, again elevating the status of women in an unhealthy and super-spiritual way.

Paul's command *"I am not permitting"* (1Timothy 2:12) suggests a pragmatic concession to a particular situation, rather than the application of a universal principle. While it is true that Paul's response to the immediate situation is not to permit women to continue teaching, the existence of women teachers in the first place underlines the fact that this ruling is a response to new circumstances – there is no reference back to an existing apostolic prohibition on women teaching, or a sense that these women were in breach of that rule.

Whereas Paul often refers back to apostolic precedent or a direct command from the Lord, such as in 1 Corinthians 11:23 where he talks about the Lord's supper saying: *"For I received from the Lord what I also passed on to you..."*, here in the passage about women teaching, he does not appeal to precedent, but simply responds to a new pastoral problem in the Ephesian church.

### *Didasko* (to teach) and *authentein* (authority)

The Greek words used for "teach" and "authority" are not all encompassing. "Teach" refers much more to the content of the teaching (here, the heretical teaching) rather than the activity of teaching in itself, while "authority" is the word used for dominate, violently lunge at (sexually) or murder. It is not a simple "be in a position of authority over". For a more detailed analysis of these two words, please refer to the appendix.

### Conclusion

The Greek used by Paul is much more specific than the conservative English translations suggest. Far from prohibiting all women from the activity of teaching any men and thus being in a position of authority over men, Paul addresses a very specific situation where wives have clearly tried to dominate their husbands and in so doing have spread false and heretical teaching. Paul's solution to this problem is to prohibit them from teaching in this context, while freely endorsing and acknowledging other women as teachers, such as Priscilla (2 Timothy 4:19), who was Apollos' teacher (Acts 18:26), and Lois and Eunice, who were Timothy's teachers.

## 2) Leadership is Male - 2 Timothy 2:2

Conservative scholars read this verse as:

*And the things you have heard me say in the presence of many witnesses entrust to reliable men (males) who will be qualified to teach others.*

### Mistranslation of *anthropos*

The Greek word used here for "men" is "*anthropos*" which is not gender specific and should more accurately be translated "people" or "mankind", both male and female, rendering the verse to read:

*And the things you have heard me say in the presence of many witnesses entrust to reliable people (anthropos) who will also be qualified to teach others.*

In the face of serious heresy, Paul instructs Timothy to entrust teaching to "faithful people" (he uses "*anthropos*" – 2 Timothy 2:2). If Paul had concern about women's suitability to teach men or anyone else, he would have specified that the teachers be male/men. Rather, his greeting to Priscilla, who was Apollos' teacher (Acts 18:26), at the end of the letter (2 Timothy 4:19), indicates that Paul recognized that women were able to teach without dominating or spreading heresy. Furthermore, his general instructions in the Epistles that believers "*teach and admonish one another in all wisdom*" (Colossians 3:16), bringing "*a lesson, a revelation, tongue or interpretation*" when meeting together (1Corinthians 14:26) cannot be limited only to men.

Therefore, to use this verse to justify a Pauline injunction to appoint only men as teachers is erroneous.

## 3) Women will be saved by childbirth – 1 Timothy 2:13-15

*13 For Adam was formed first, then Eve. 14 And Adam was not the one deceived; it was the woman who was deceived and became a sinner. 15 But women will be saved through childbearing—if they continue in faith, love and holiness with propriety.*

This verse has been used by ultra conservatives to suggest that women must give birth in order to be saved or spiritually effective. This contradicts the biblical principle of free grace in Christ for everyone. We cannot say that Paul was stating that women MUST have children in order to be fully accepted in Christ – as where would that leave barren married women or singles – and Paul endorses singleness in his letter to the Corinthians. Paul boldly argues all through his writing to the Jewish legalists that only faith in the atonement of Christ ever brings true conversion and salvation.

So what does this verse mean? Scholars differ in their opinion! Paul makes many references in his pastoral epistles to endless genealogies (1Timothy 1:4; 2 Timothy 4:4; Titus 1:10-14) and these reflect gnostic interest in the knowledge of origins, which was thought to bring salvation. One of the gnostic heresies was that Eve was created first and was Adam's mother (his origin) and the mother of all living things. That is why Paul emphasizes that Adam (not Eve) was formed first. Furthermore, the opposition of the false teachers to marriage and childbirth (1Timothy 4:2, 5:14) also reflects some gnostic views that regarded it as impossible for women to gain eternal life whilst retaining a female identity and capacity to bear children. Kroeger suggests that this verse addresses this gnostic heresy, and instructs women not to deny their femininity and the natural desire for children in order to find their salvation. It is likely that Paul wanted to affirm the calling of women as mothers and endorse childbearing as just as "spiritual".

However, other scholars believe that the Greek text refers to the Messiah who was born of the Virgin Mary.

Since the Greek language does not have punctuation, which usually helps us to define the emphasis or meaning, some interpretation of the text's meaning is always required. So this verse could equally be translated in this way:

*But women will be saved through the bearing of THE CHILD (i.e. the Christ Child).*

So, just as a woman (Eve) was part of the Fall, so a woman (Mary) was part of the story of Redemption and Salvation.

Or another translation could be:

*She will be saved by the Child bearing.*

Scholar Katharine Bushnell in a study in 1923 wrote concerning this verse:

*"Women are not literally saved from all death during childbirth nor are they saved spiritually by the mere animal process of birthing. Women are saved from their sins on the same terms as men as God is no respecter of persons. The literal translation from the Greek is 'She (woman) shall be saved by THE child bearing' – that is, by the birth of a Redeemer into the world."*[4]

---

[4] Bushnell, Katharine *God's Word to Women*, Published via reprint, ed. Ray Munson, 1976

## 4) Head covering for women - 1 Corinthians 11:3-16

*Now I want you to realize that the head of every man is Christ, and the head of the woman is man, and the head of Christ is God. 4 Every man who prays or prophesies with his head covered dishonours his head. 5 And every woman who prays or prophesies with her head uncovered dishonours her head—it is just as though her head were shaved. 6 If a woman does not cover her head, she should have her hair cut off; and if it is a disgrace for a woman to have her hair cut or shaved off, she should cover her head. 7 A man ought not to cover his head since he is the image and glory of God; but the woman is the glory of man. 8 For man did not come from woman, but woman from man; 9 neither was man created for woman, but woman for man. 10 For this reason, and because of the angels, the woman ought to have a sign of authority on her head. 11 In the Lord, however, woman is not independent of man, nor is man independent of woman. 12 For as woman came from man, so also man is born of woman. But everything comes from God. 13 Judge for yourselves: Is it proper for a woman to pray to God with her head uncovered? 14 Does not the very nature of things teach you that if a man has long hair, it is a disgrace to him, 15 but that if a woman has long hair, it is her glory? For long hair is given to her as a covering. 16 If anyone wants to be contentious about this, we have no other practice—nor do the churches of God.*

This scripture is one of the most complex and many scholars admit that they do not fully understand its context or allusion to the angels enough to be confident that they have fully understood the true intention here. In spite of this widely acknowledged ambiguity, this scripture has been used to validate the need for women to have appropriate "covering" for them to minister. Some traditions have taken this literally and insist on a literal head covering, shawl or veil, while others have interpreted this figuratively and applied it to the need for a wife to function under the spiritual "covering" or authority of her husband. Some have gone still further and maintain that this passage sets out a hierarchical "chain of command" where men have authority (headship) over women, taking the Greek word for "head" (*kephale*) to mean authority as we use head in the English such as the head of state, headmaster or head of the army, i.e. implying rule, authority and a sense of being "the boss".

Greek scholars, however, argue that *"kephale"* hardly ever implied these meanings in any Greek usage of the day. Had Paul meant "head" as we use it in the English to convey leadership and authority, he would have used the word *"arche"* which is unambiguous in the Greek, whereas *"kephale"* usually meant "source" such as in "head of the river" or "source of being" rather than head as in leader. The only place where *"kephale"* was used in the military for example, it meant the front line or exposed position but did not convey senior rank. In Colossians 1:18 Paul refers to Christ as the "head" of his body, the church, in a context that implies he is the source of its being. If Paul had meant to convey authority he would most likely have chosen a number of other words in the Greek so as to avoid any chance of confusion. The only place *"exousia"* (authority) is mentioned is in 1 Corinthians 11:10 in relation to the woman's own authority.

It is evident from this passage here that Paul's line of argument suggests that he is addressing several cultural issues which are more obscure to us in our context today but were nevertheless clearly concerns in his day. Paul divides his reasoning into (a) arguments from the honour/shame culture; (b) arguments from creation; and finally (c) arguments from propriety and decency.[5] Underlying each of these arguments is a clear exhortation to the church to prevent the gospel becoming an unnecessary stumbling block because of the new freedom enjoyed by Christians. Paul encourages the Corinthian women to observe the cultural traditions of the day, of their own free will, in order not to bring shame on their husbands and so discredit themselves and their faith.

## a)  An argument from the honour/shame culture
   ## 1 Corinthians 11:3-6

Paul's point is nothing to do with women's subordination, but rather with a practice among the women of the day (which we do not know in detail) which had brought shame on that culture and so Paul was reinforcing the need to exercise restraint in order not to bring shame on others or on oneself. Commentators suggest there were issues around the blurring of sexual and gender distinctiveness in physical appearance, with men wearing their hair long, while women shaved their heads instead of having their natural covering of hair. This

---

[5] This and what follows is a summary of the argument outlined by Gordon Fee [Prof of NT, Regent College, Vancouver], in his excellent commentary on 1 Corinthians (*The First Epistle to the Corinthians*, The New International Commentary on the NT, Eerdmans, 1987)

made some assume they were temple prostitutes which shamed their husbands and themselves and therefore also reflected poorly on the Gospel. Set in the context of chapters 8-10, the passage appears to reflect Paul's on-going concern that individual freedom be limited for the sake of unity within the church (1Corinthians 8:9; 10:23-30), effective witness outside it (1 Corinthians 9:22), and concern for the glory of God (1Corinthians 10:31-11:1).

Paul opens this passage with praise for the Corinthian Christians (verse 2) for keeping the traditions of the day. Paul then creates the theological construct using "head" metaphorically in relation to three relationships: man/Christ; woman/man; Christ/God (verse 3). He then goes on to describe two kinds of covering or hairstyle (verses 4-5a), where the "head" from verse 3 will be shamed by the man's or woman's actions.

Paul then elaborates specifically in relation to the woman's actions where the shame reflects both on the man as well as on herself; Paul argues that for both the covering should be maintained. Paul wants to shift the argument from one of personal freedom (which women now have in Christ) to one of relational responsibility in the culture of the day. In all of this, his concern is to remove any stumbling block to the Gospel, rather than to lay down a universal principle. He does the same in relation to eating food sacrificed to idols, for example, and says that, with the freedom Christians have, they should decide based on conscience what they will eat but be prepared to voluntarily limit this freedom if someone else's faith or the Gospel is at stake. *Be careful, however, that the exercise of your rights does not become a stumbling block to the weak.* (1 Corinthians 8:9) It is the same line of argument here in relation to head coverings.

There is no sense at all in the passage that what Paul establishes here is a hierarchical structure of authority. "Thus Paul's concern is not hierarchical (who has authority over whom), but relational (the unique relationships that are predicated on one's being the source of the other's existence)." (G. Fee) "Head" or "*kephale*" is therefore an indication of the man's social pre-eminence or prominence in a patriarchal society which lends women social status by virtue of their married status, as in many Middle Eastern nations today. In this sense a man was very much the "source" of a woman's being and without him she had no status. This emphasizes how remarkable Jesus' treatment of women was, conveying on them status by virtue of who they were, rather than who their husband was.

### b) An argument from creation
### 1 Corinthians 11:7-12

Paul seems to refer to the creation account in Genesis 2 and highlights that woman was created for man, bone from his bone etc. As he is her "head" (origin, source of life), she is his glory which is why she should not shame him through any behaviour which would erode their distinctiveness and gift, one to another. Paul thus comments on the status quo in the society, or the accepted societal norms.

However, as frequently in his writings, he then goes beyond the status quo and adds the radical Gospel commentary which expects higher standards than the societal norm. In verses 11-12 Paul describes that, just as woman came from man, so man is born from woman and both come from God, so emphasizing equality "in the Lord" rather than subordination, but also stressing inter-dependence.

### c) An argument from propriety
### 1 Corinthians 11:13-16

Paul reverts back to his discussion of head covering, discussing now the propriety of having long hair for women and short hair for men as is "natural" or the common practice in society at the time. The fact that his appeal is to common practice, not to a regulation or requirement as such, emphasizes his earlier argument about the expected norm which can bring honour or shame. This then means that Paul's final appeal, beginning with "judge for yourselves", concludes the argument on this issue with an appeal to one's own sense of propriety and authority to judge what is appropriate. Whereas in other epistles on other matters he is perfectly capable of stating an injunction or command of God, here he is simply appealing for right behaviour based on the acceptable cultural practices.

### And finally because of the angels...
### 1 Corinthians 11:10

> For this reason, and because of (through the enabling of) the angels, the woman ought to have (a sign) of authority (on) over her head.

While most scholars acknowledge the difficulties with the head coverings passage, all are agreed that verse 10 is the most obscure in the New Testament. The reference to angels is a mystery which many have attempted to shed light on, few with any confidence and all conceding that we cannot fully understand this without knowing the exact context of Paul's comments.

However, what is easier to comment on is the phrase "a sign of authority on her head" or "authority over her head". Traditional readings have explained that the sign is a sign of authority or power which the husband has over his wife through the symbol of the veil or head covering. However, on closer examination we can see that this meaning is not true to the original Greek. The word used for authority is *"exousia"*, a term used to express our own power, rather than the power exercised by another over us. So, in this context, it is a word to describe the woman's own authority/power over her head, rather than the husband's.

The verse could therefore read:

*For this reason, and because of (through the enabling of) the angels, the woman ought to have (a sign) of (her own) authority (on) over her head.*

This would render this verse to mean that the veil is a symbol signifying the woman's own authority, presumably through her free choice to wear the covering out of deference to the cultural expectation of propriety and decency and so as not to shame her husband.

## 5) Women should remain silent - 1 Corinthians 14:33b-36

*For God is not a God of disorder but of peace—as in all the congregations of the Lord's people. **34** Women should remain silent in the churches. They are not allowed to speak, but must be in submission, as the law says. **35** If they want to inquire about something, they should ask their own husbands at home; for it is disgraceful for a woman to speak in the church. **36** Or did the word of God originate with you? Or are you the only people it has reached?*

This passage has caused great confusion among commentators and scholars. Far from being as straightforward as our English translations suggest, the Greek original text is far more ambiguous and seems to contradict all other Pauline writings. This has led some scholars to suggest that the passage is not original to Paul, but a later addition/interpolation which was incorporated into later manuscripts. Other scholars who accept Pauline authorship and also recognize Paul's call for women to be silent see this prohibition as relating to certain kinds of speech. They point to the context of the passage, which suggests that Paul's concern is once again related to good order in public worship. While the exact situation that Paul is addressing remains unclear, his goal in writing is to give three instructions to prevent disorder: relating to those speaking in tongues (14:27-8), those prophesying (14:29-32) and to women or wives (14:34a). All three groups are commanded to be silent in specific situations, suggesting that none of the prohibitions are permanent.

If Paul has a specific context in mind, how should his rare appeal to "the Law" be understood (1Corinthians

14:34)? There is no reference in Mosaic Law (Torah) to women being quiet in the assembly so Paul cannot be referring to a particular verse or quote in the Law of Moses. However, some scholars allude to the references in the Talmud which do express this sentiment about women being silent. The Talmud was the Jewish oral law that the Scribes and Pharisees had interpreted from their understanding of the Torah. The Talmud, which began to be written down after 70 AD, contains the opinions of thousands of rabbis on a variety of subjects, including law, ethics, philosophy, customs, history, theology and many other topics. The Talmud is the basis for all codes of rabbinic law and is much quoted in other rabbinic literature. It became the Jewish rule book and guide for conduct and etiquette. So it seems likely that Paul's reference relates to Jewish customs or general traditions within society, his missionary concerns making it important to please everybody, causing neither Greeks nor Jews to stumble so that all may be saved (1 Corinthians 10:32, 33). To avoid causing disgrace in the shame/honour culture, women are to follow the social order that is observed in other contemporary churches (14:33,40), learning from their husbands at home, though Paul seems to warn against legalism by challenging his hearers not to impose the Talmudic law above the word of God itself.

On this basis, an alternate approach to the passage has recently been proposed by Bilezikian, who suggests that verses 33-35 are not Paul's own opinions but those of a group within the church. As he does elsewhere in the letter, Paul quotes the opinions of his opponents in order to refute them with the emphatic participle "*ē*" ("or", translated "what!" in RSV) that introduces verse 36. Bilezikian suggests that these teachers are Judaizers, indicated in part by the content of the teaching and also the fact that they come from the "congregations of the saints" (14:33b), an early designation for churches of Jewish Christians established in Jerusalem and Palestine.

Bilezikian suggests that Paul's response (verses 36-39) further indicates his disapproval of silencing women. He sees Paul as sarcastically asking if God's word is given to "just you men" (verse 36) challenging anyone claiming prophetic gifting to exercise it and so see that Paul's teaching is based on that of Christ (verse 37), not the law[6]. Anyone not recognizing Paul's authority in this matter should be rejected (verse 38). As the main theme of the passage is that all should be done "in a fitting and orderly way" (verse 40), they should "eagerly desire to prophesy" and "not forbid speaking in tongues" (verse 39).

The sentence structure, lacking in punctuation as was usual in the Greek, might suggest that Paul is quoting local commentary or discussion amongst the men. We would usually have quotation marks to indicate what is a quote and what is our own statement but in the Greek no such punctuation exists and has to be inferred from the text.

So this would mean that the verses could read as follows:

---

[6] "...Paul is quoting derisively the words of his Judeo-Christian opponents", Bilezikian, *Beyond Sex Roles: A Guide for the Study of Female Roles in the Bible* (3rd ed. 2006)

*As in all the congregations of the saints (i.e. Jewish congregations), (you say that) women should remain silent (behave quietly) in the churches. They are not allowed to speak (have a long argument), but must be in submission, as the (Talmud) Law says. (As the Talmud dictates you say) 'If they want to enquire about something, they should ask their own husbands at home; for it is disgraceful for a woman to speak (have a long argument) in the church.' (But I say) Did the word of God originate with you? Or are you the only people it has reached?*

As is clear from the discussions amongst scholars, this passage is by no means straightforward, even if read literally, as the literal Greek is unclear. In the sweep of Scripture and other Pauline writing where Paul very clearly endorses women's participation, for example by prophesying, it is not wise to take this one passage and create a theology which forbids women from speaking in church.

## 6) Women as the weaker partner - 1 Peter 3:7

**1 Peter 3:7**
*Husbands, in the same way be considerate as you live with your wives, and treat them with respect as the weaker* (Gk *asthenes*) *partner and as heirs with you of the gracious gift of life, so that nothing will hinder your prayers.*

This Greek word "*asthenes*", translated as "weaker", does not portray the sense that a woman is weaker in wisdom, spirituality or any sense of being a lesser partner. This word weaker just means, literally, a vessel made from weaker fabric or weaker structure. This just refers to the physical vessel, or outer body, stating that husbands should be considerate and live with an awareness that their wife may be weaker in her physical frame. In other words, husbands, be considerate – take note that your wife has a weaker fabric physically and so treat her with honour and respect. There is no sense given by the use of this word "weaker" that she is lesser in any area of life or function but just different in her physical construct.

Peter here was addressing a cultural issue and pleading with men to treat their wives in a kind and considerate manner. Anyone who has lived in the Middle East or Asia would be familiar with the custom where a husband would feel very comfortable to walk empty-handed and carry nothing, walking a few metres in front of his wife who then struggles behind him carrying all the shopping piled on her head while leading the animals. With this picture in mind you will be able to visualize more clearly that Peter is reminding these husbands that they should not consider their wives as their "third donkey" and make them their beast of burden. He is actually asking husbands to be more tender and considerate; this is not a slur against women-kind calling them "weak", as some women have felt.

Peter also highlights the fact that a wrong relationship with your wife could be a hindrance in your relationship with God and in seeing your prayers answered. Here Peter is telling the husbands that they should expect the health of their spiritual lives to be impacted if they are inconsiderate towards their wives. He explains to them that they need to include their wives as *"joint heirs with them of the gracious gift of life"*. This respectful treatment of a wife by a husband will ultimately bless the husband with answered prayers and spiritual breakthroughs!

# 5 Answering more tough questions!

Now we begin to move on to another controversial area where we discuss the role of women as leaders in the church. We will face the tough questions head on, we will examine the difficult texts and attempt to present an overview of the various opinions and finally conclude with our understanding of them. Unfortunately, there is no definitive proof and universally agreed conclusion to many of these arguments, hence the continuing disagreements about this whole area of women in leadership and their defined role within the church. If any of these arguments could be definitely established with certainty someone would already have done it! So we will just present our journey of understanding on these tricky and difficult topics. Please be patient with us as we try to explore these questions!

## Why were no women included with the 12 apostles?

It is often suggested by conservative theologians that if God had intended women to be equal with men in the ministry, Jesus would have had women in his core team.

But could there be another reason why the first apostles were only men?

**Prophetic Stance**: Several scholars explain that the choice of twelve men was a prophetic and symbolic choice. This was to demonstrate the birthing of the new Kingdom. The number 12 always represents the government of God's kingdom. So Jesus was making a prophetic statement to the leaders of the Jewish people by choosing twelve men to represent the twelve tribes of Israel with its origins in the sons of Jacob. Twelve Jewish men exactly mirrored the original twelve patriarchs and demonstrated the fulfilment of Messianic prophecy through Jesus.

By selecting men He was saying to the Scribes and Pharisees that He was creating a "New Israel". He was sending them out to "the lost sheep of the tribes of Israel" to serve in a symbolic, foundational role to reach the Jews with a message. So, although men were chosen, in this instance it was symbolic, not a sexist statement, nor was Jesus denying women a future role in His church as is clearly evidenced when He chose a woman to be the first to testify to the resurrection.

It might also be noted that Jesus' choice of apostles was limited to Jews and did not include Gentiles though no one argues that this sets a precedent for only having church leaders of Jewish descent today! Again, this was not an action by Jesus to set a universal precedent but rather a choice to demonstrate the fulfilment of prophecy which said that a Messiah would come and be sent to the lost sheep of Israel. To add Gentiles and women to that initial group of twelve would have meant losing the prophetic picture. Once the signpost had been set up, however, Jesus' model and actions became inclusive of both men and women. The Cross broke down all dividing walls so that Galatians 3:28 could be established: *There is neither Jew nor Gentile, neither slave nor free, nor is there male and female, for you are all one in Christ Jesus.*[7]

***Cultural Stance:*** If we look at the culture of the day, women were not allowed to occupy any positions of authority and for them to do so in the Jewish and Roman culture would have been so radical as to be a stumbling block to Jesus' mission. However, once the prophetic statement explained above had been made, Jesus subverted tradition in choosing and commissioning women to be His witnesses, affirming their spiritual insights and allowing them to follow Him. Luke 10:38 affirms Mary's decision to "sit at Jesus' feet" while her sister Martha was busy in the kitchen. The phrase to sit at someone's feet was the commonly understood expression of being a disciple, later used, for example, by Paul who said he was "brought up at the feet of Gamaliel" (Acts 22:3). So there is no doubt that what Jesus was allowing Mary to do by sitting at his feet was be given equal place with the other disciples. Jesus' choice of women to be the first witnesses to the resurrection, in spite of the fact that the testimony of a woman in that culture was considered unreliable, encapsulated the redemption message where every curse is broken, including that which divides the genders.

---

[7] For a fuller discussion of this topic look at Bailey, Dr Kenneth E. *"Women in the New Testament: A Middle Eastern Cultural View."*, ANVIL Journal, 1994 and Bilezikain, Dr. Gilbert *Why Jesus Chose Male Apostles* in *Community 101: Reclaiming the local Church as Community of Oneness,* Zondervan 1997.

## So what about women as elders and apostles today?

"What do you call yourself, what is your title, Rachel?" I am asked this question again and again. Some people do call me prophetic while others may call me pathetic! Some would say I am an evangelist, while others claim I have apostolic gifting. So who do I say that I am? Well, I call myself Rachel! I personally believe that we do not give ourselves titles, whether male or female, but they are given to us. Both God and mankind give positions and titles to people. Some women get very offended as they feel that their gift is not being recognized with the appropriate position and title just because they are a woman. I do understand this sense of injustice but I still do not advocate this as a wise path to tread. I would rather not fight this battle and let people and God give me my name. After all, we are not doing what we are doing for names and titles but surely we serve because we love Jesus and His is the greatest name of all!

From social reformers to senior registrars in hospitals, from the boardrooms of companies to head teachers in schools, women hold positions of leadership at every level of society. In the Kingdom women have often been pioneers, especially in missions contexts, but when it comes to church leadership there is often a hesitation as regards the appropriate place for women with leadership gifts.

As we consider this question, we must first clarify that, depending on our churchmanship and culture, we may or may not consider this question relevant. In certain Western denominations, church structure does not include elders and no one would be called an apostle. There may even be an assumption that apostles only exist in Africa or Asia where such titles are used more, although even there often the function and responsibility attached to the same title would differ from culture to culture and nation to nation. I will never forget meeting a 19-year-old Chinese woman who had been preaching the Gospel since she was 15 and was now overseeing 600 churches. She was introduced to me as the apostle for this region in the underground church since she had performed many miracles and planted these churches!

Implicit in this question then, whether or not the word elder, overseer, bishop or apostle is used, is the wider question of should a woman be in a senior leadership role and potentially be in a position where she has oversight or authority over men. As we have already seen, biblical examples abound of women functioning in a variety of roles including a judge (Deborah), a prophet (Huldah), a church leader (Priscilla) and many co-workers of Paul. Jesus chose a woman to be the first witness entrusted with the good news that He had risen from the dead, and this in a culture which considered the testimony of a woman to be worthless. The early church had women apostles in its ranks, notably Junia who is mentioned in Scripture. And yet today this issue is often the most controversial of all.

## Why so controversial?

Part of the challenge connected with this issue is less to do with gender and much more a reflection on our understanding of leadership itself. Many of our church structures are set up hierarchically and so senior leadership implies being at the top of the pyramid rather than fulfilling a function in the church. While it is not possible for us to fully tackle the subject of biblical authority and leadership within the remit of our current discussion in this book, we will make just a few comments here for your own further reflection.

## A matter of gifting not gender

Current equality legislation in the West has forced the issue of equal gender representation, so much so that at times there has been an unhelpful pressure to include a "token" woman on every board or committee, whatever their competence. This does not truly recognize the call of the person to the role but rather promotes a woman solely to meet a quota. In Scripture, leadership is never a right but rather a grace gift given to some. This means that not all women, or for that matter men, will have this specific ability nor should they demand a role for the sake of equal opportunity. Instead, the sense of Scripture is that those evidencing a clear God-given anointing, coupled always with godly character, should be permitted to exercise their gift for the good of the whole. The qualification for ministry is not firstly your gender, but your character and calling, whether male or female.

**Romans 12:6-8 (NLT)**
*In his grace, God has given us different gifts for doing certain things well. So if God has given you the ability to prophesy, speak out with as much faith as God has given you. 7 If your gift is serving others, serve them well. If you are a teacher, teach well. 8 If your gift is to encourage others, be encouraging. If it is giving, give generously. If God has given you leadership ability, take the responsibility seriously. And if you have a gift for showing kindness to others, do it gladly.*

If as a woman you know before God you have been given leadership abilities but yet you are not released to lead in the church, this can become a source of great frustration. How can a woman take her responsibility seriously, as exhorted by this scripture, if she is not allowed to serve as a leader within the church? This barrier of acceptance has often caused outstanding women leaders to use their skills in the secular world, where they are recognized and encouraged, rather than in the church.

## A matter of tasks not titles

Paul also speaks of the gifts of apostle, prophet, pastor, teacher and evangelist not in the context of titles and positions but rather as gifts given to the church to make her mature and to get a job done.

**Ephesians 4:11-12 (NLT)**
*Now these are the gifts Christ gave to the church: the apostles, the prophets, the evangelists, and the pastors and teachers. 12 Their responsibility is to equip God's people to do his work and build up the church, the body of Christ.*

I love the motto of a church I know in South Africa which says "Your success, my honour". The emphasis of both passages above is of a gift given to serve the church to make her shine and help her achieve her mission. Gender is not mentioned at all.

Alan Vincent, in his study "What does God say about women", explains what an apostle actually was. Here we quote some of his study: *"The word apostle literally means 'the sent one'. It comes in a verbal form many times as apostellō which means 'to send'. As Alexander*

69

the Great was advancing his kingdom, he would send out military expeditions. The purpose of this military expedition was to conquer certain territory and bring it under the rule and government of the king. A military commander was put in charge and he was called an apostle. The company of armed soldiers that went with him were called an apostolic band.

By the time we come to Jesus' life and the time of the writing of the New Testament these words were well in place and this was their meaning. These words mean to be **sent by someone who has great authority**. Under their authority you are sent as a commander of an expeditionary force. The purpose is to extend the boundaries of the kingdom. You go there as a warring community to conquer and establish the rule of the king in an area where that rule is not yet established.

Many have problems seeing a woman functioning apostolically in her own right. They can recognize the principle of apostolic partnership like Priscilla and Aquila, but believe that the man gives the credibility to the woman's functioning alongside. They worked together as a father and mother to build and nurture churches. However they struggle to see how the woman can function on her own in this position.

I am totally convinced that women can be apostles and many of the warrior generals that God is raising up today are women. We must recognize that they are the sent ones of the Lord and receive the gift they represent. These women are sent to conquer in the name of the Lord and to establish the kingdom by the power of their warring ability. They will be leading an army of generals.

*I want us to agree together that we will not prevent these great warrior apostles from coming forth, whether male or female, whether single or married. These things do not stop the legitimacy of their ministry and function in the body of Christ. The final test of the scriptural truth we are talking about is the witness of the Holy Spirit."*

## Women in Church history

Many of the major pioneers and missionaries in the last centuries have been women. They were apostles, literally "sent out ones", who planted churches and transformed communities. Recent examples include Jackie Pullinger in Hong Kong and Heidi Baker in Mozambique. Women also make up around 70% of the Chinese underground church planting leadership, many of whom are still under 30 years old and unmarried.

Women have also been major pioneers throughout history and have contributed to the reform of our prisons, health and welfare services, the statutory conditions of the work place, and our attitudes towards slavery and other forms of injustice. Florence Nightingale, Elizabeth Fry and Emily Pankhurst all stood as reformers in their day and changed the landscape of our nations.

**Conclusion:**

The overwhelming evidence from Scripture as well as church history demonstrates that women have been and were included at every level of church and social leadership, with some even acting as military leaders and judges. These women do not fit a particular mould: some are married, others single, some minister alongside their husbands while others clearly exercised authority in their own right and were honoured and respected for it, with no evidence to suggest that their role was only secure or practised under "male headship".

# 6 Headship, covering and male authority issues!

Should women take a leadership role, especially if men are present? What should be the correct authority structure when you have a man and a woman working together? Are women inferior to men governmentally? What about covering and submission issues? What is the appropriate conduct for women in their relationship with other men? Why do so many theologians argue against women taking leadership roles and insist that the Bible teaches the need for male headship? In order to tackle these questions we need to understand the curse of the Fall and its consequences for the relationship between men and women.

## Bitter war is declared between Satan, the Woman and her seed

There has always been a battle raging between the sexes and an inequality of gender which has acted as a curse on relationships between men and women. Many have mistakenly argued that God's divine creation order instituted male leadership and female submission. However, a closer look at the creation narratives reveals that God's creation was in His image, "*male and female He created them*" (Genesis 1:27). In this, both man and woman reflect the image of God and there is no hint of one gender superseding the other. The only suggestion of hierarchy comes as a result of the Fall. In Genesis 3, the curse of the Fall is that man will toil and labour for a living (Genesis 3:17-19), thus connecting his identity, existence and survival with his work, while the woman is told "*your desire will be for your husband and he will **rule over** you*" (3:16). Woman's identity becomes wrapped up in that of her husband and this illegitimate need results in his domination and "rule" over her.

While the Bible clearly states that this will be the case, Scripture does not institute this as God's original design or intention. Far from this being the created order, God allows man and woman to suffer the consequences of their choices and the curse of their sin. As a result of their disobedience, both are judged in their own right and discordance enters their relationship. Where God's original plan was for equal and joint rulership over creation (Genesis 1:26 *Then God said, 'Let us make man in our image, in our likeness, and let **them** rule over the fish of the sea and the birds of the air, over the livestock, over all the earth, and over all the creatures that move along the ground.'*), the Fall establishes the rule of man over woman. Only the cross could break this curse and Paul emphasizes this when he says that now in Christ *there is neither…male nor female for you are all one in Christ.* (Galatians 3:28) 1 Peter 3:7 reaffirms joint authority in encouraging husbands to treat their wives as *heirs with you of the gracious gift of life.*

**Ephesians 2:14-15**

*For he himself is our peace, who has made the two groups one and has destroyed the barrier, the dividing wall of hostility, 15 by setting aside in his flesh the law with its commands and regulations. His purpose was to create in himself one new humanity out of the two, thus making peace,*

The dividing walls of hostility between male and female are abolished in Christ, but only if we are willing to allow God to set us free from any alignment with the oppressive agenda of the enemy. Genesis 3:15 then also speaks of a special enmity between Satan and womankind. This enmity between the devil and women is manifested in many attacks that undermine a woman's identity, purpose and call, leaving her feeling crushed and isolated. Religious spirits (whether they are through Islam, Hinduism, Judaism or the Church) particularly target women and the result of this oppressive atmosphere is misogyny, patriarchy and the suppression of women. Whether as a result of ignorance or deception, poor theology or blind prejudice, we need to be careful that we do not align with the post-Fall curse rather than God's original and pure design. For those of us who have simply inherited our theology from others without actually studying the Scriptures for ourselves, we need to be willing to reassess our theological stance and ask the tough questions of ourselves and of Scripture and allow the Holy Spirit to correct us.

Above all, we need to understand that a spiritual battle rages over this issue.

## Authority Issues

**Matthew 20:25-28**

*Jesus called them together and said, "You know that the rulers of the Gentiles lord it over them, and their high officials exercise authority over them. 26 Not so with you. Instead, whoever wants to become great among you must be your servant, 27 and whoever wants to be first must be your slave — 28 just as the Son of Man did not come to be served, but to serve, and to give his life as a ransom for many."*

As this Scripture demonstrates, we need to model Christ-like leadership which always lifts up and never tears down. So the Kingdom never has a system of hierarchy but of honouring one another. The whole idea of greater and lesser is man's way of thinking, not God's. After the Fall, Jesus comes to restore all things – surely this must include men and women to their correct partnership.

## Misunderstanding of Headship

As I read Gordon's response to an angry email, I had to smile. Gordon had not taken the complaint from an offended Canadian minister very seriously. This man had written to him complaining that I had had the audacity to speak and teach leaders at a seminar in Winnipeg, Canada, and did I not understand that the scriptures prohibit this? He then asked why Gordon was happy to allow me to minister, dishonouring his covering and headship, and laid out his opinion of our marriage and Gordon's character. Finally he concluded: "And to top it all Rachel even ministered in PANTS – this was the final straw for me!" But dear Gordon had not reacted to the slur on his leadership and had written back to this man graciously. He explained that I was ministering with his blessing and encouragement and that Christ was my head and he was happy. He then stated: "And finally I must point out that I always insist that Rachel wears PANTS when she ministers. I would be horrified if she ministered without her pants on. She was honouring me when she did this!" (For the UK English readers, pants from the Canadian pastor meant trousers and, for the USA readers, pants from Gordon meant my underwear!)

Sometimes we can get too political and angry about these matters and lose our grace unnecessarily. At all times, even if we disagree, we should still be friends and have a good laugh!!

**Ephesians 5: 21-27**
*Submit to one another out of reverence for Christ. 22 Wives, submit to your husbands as to the Lord. 23 For the husband is the head of the wife as Christ is the head of the church, his body, of which he is the Saviour. 24 Now as the church submits to Christ, so also wives should submit to their husbands in everything. 25 Husbands, love your wives, just as Christ loved the church and gave himself up for her 26 to make her holy, cleansing her by the washing with water through the word, 27 and to present her to himself as a radiant church, without stain or wrinkle or any other blemish, but holy and blameless.*

There is a misconception that the Bible says ALL women should submit to ALL men. Proponents of male headship in marriage have traditionally seen the Ephesians passage, which addresses husband and wife, as starting in verse 22 with the command to wives to submit to their husbands. Male headship is then developed to argue the case for a husband to be the decision-maker in the home as "head" is defined as "the leader" or "the boss". Spiritually, headship in marriage is also seen to bestow on the husband the role of being the priest in his home, taking spiritual responsibility and leadership. The question which must therefore be considered is whether the theology of headship in marriage can legitimately be derived from this Ephesians passage and then verified by other examples of God's dealing with men and women elsewhere in the Bible.

Purely on the basis of the flow of these verses in Ephesians, a mistake occurs in many conservative translations of the Bible which emphasize a wife's submission to her husband by placing a break in the chapter after verse 21, and before verse 22, thus breaking the flow of the verses and disconnecting the command to wives from the previous command to both parties to "*submit to one another*" in verse 21. The original Greek does not have this break and, in fact, the passage flows as one sentence from verse 18 with the encouragement to be filled with the Holy Spirit, out of which these verses then flow, starting with mutual submission and elaborating on what that means for each party.

## Submission versus Obedience

Secondly, linguistically there is a difference in Greek between submission and obedience. Obedience, in its absolute sense, is when a military command is given. You simply say: "Yes, Sir!" That is only used in terms of our relationship to God. Jesus Himself, in his (submitted) humanity, obeyed God the Father. Everything His Father said he obeyed without questioning.

However, in every other relationship, that same Greek word for obedience is never used. Unfortunately, the words are translated the same way in our English Bible so that the distinction is not properly made. The Greek word used for submit is *"hupotasso"* which means "to put yourself under the authority of". This means that we recognize the relationship that has authority upon us, but we are not required to blindly obey but rather voluntarily put ourselves under its authority. In relation to God we obey; in relation to a husband we are called to submit. Nowhere in scripture is blind obedience ever implied. True submission is a voluntary gift you give – it cannot be demanded from you. You can submit even to those who do not deserve it – like Jesus submitting to (though not obeying!) Pilate – as it is your choice to give your respect and honour to a socially recognized authority. Submission was never intended to humiliate you, but bless you. It should lift your head up, not make you feel crushed. You choose to serve and give your life to honour others and the security of the relationship brings you blessing.

## Why the distinction in marriage?

If Paul is constantly arguing the case for mutual submission and equal partnership between men and women, why does he seem to make a distinction between husbands and wives and emphasize that wives should submit? This is a question scholars always address as it is often used as the pattern for male headship authority and the requirement for a man's covering in order for a wife to be seen as "submitted".

The most common explanation given by scholars is that Paul is operating within the social household codes of his day. Here it was the cultural norm for a husband to be the "boss" in the home and demand obedience of everyone within the home from slaves to children and including his wife. Just as in many parts of the Middle East today, the husband's authority would have been absolute, with no room for debate, and this often led to harsh treatment of slaves, abuse of wives and an atmosphere of fear in which children were raised. So the context of Paul's comments in Ephesians falls within comments about household codes, covering three pairs of relationships, namely husbands and wives (5:21-33), parents and children (6:1-4) and slaves and masters (6:6-9). In each of these cases, Paul recognizes the limitation of the prevailing household codes and does not seek to overturn them completely. He doesn't, for example, ban slavery, though this does not mean that he advocates it either. But what he does do is recognize that certain codes and situations do exist and that these need reforming in Spirit-filled homes. So in the case of masters he advises good treatment of slaves; in the case of children he exhorts fathers not to exasperate their offspring; and in the case of husbands he instructs them to love their wives as themselves. But Paul also exhorts the traditionally socially disadvantaged party within each relationship and encourages them to honour and respect those whom society has placed over them, not so much because they have to obey, but because they choose to give as if it were "unto the Lord". So, in the case of children, Paul says they should honour their parents and, in the case of slaves, they should work diligently in the sight of the Lord rather than just when their masters are watching over them.

So it is that in this context Paul begins to address the marriage relationship. Here his guidelines are equally radical. He begins in verse 21 by stating equality or parity in the sight of God: *"submit **to one another** out of reverence for Christ"*. He then addresses the wives and encourages them to submit to their husbands. This is a request that she should voluntarily choose to submit herself to the socially recognized authority who is her husband. He does not command her to obey but to submit, following the example of Jesus who submitted Himself to the authorities over Him. Paul then turns his attention to husbands and, as an outworking of the same verse 21 where he asks that Christians submit one to another, he asks husbands to love their wives. No such injunction existed in the household codes of the day. A wife was her husband's property and he could choose to do whatever he wanted with her. She had no rights, nor status of her own and certainly could not expect love or respect. For Paul to therefore compare the husband with Christ, and ask the husband to model himself on Jesus' sacrificial laying down of His life for the Church, was astonishingly radical. In effect Paul was overturning the husband's right to do as he pleased, instead requiring selfless sacrifice and love.

Far from instituting a hierarchical authority structure in the home with the husband as the head in the sense of the boss or leader, Paul's words actually go quite some way to dismantling the patriarchal nature of household relationships and placing husband and wife much more on a level with each other. However, as a concession to the culture and "social norms", and for the sake of unity and harmony in the home as well as presenting the

Gospel in a good light in the honour/shame culture of the day, Paul exhorts husband and wife to each surrender some of their freedoms: the husband should voluntarily surrender some of his socially bestowed "rights" and learn to love his wife as he loves himself (verse 33), while the wife, who has discovered her new God-given value and equality, should voluntarily surrender some of that freedom and choose to submit to her husband as to the Lord[8].

But what then of Paul's use of the word "head" and how should this headship be understood? Does this socially conferred headship also assume spiritual leadership? Before we can come to a conclusion on the relationship between headship and spiritual leadership in marriage, we need to look at a broader spectrum of illustration of marriage in the Bible for clarity. One example within the early church is found in Acts 5:1-11 and the case of Ananias and Sapphira. According to traditional proponents of male headship authority in marriage, by virtue of Ananias' headship, and on the basis that, as the husband he would be responsible for the decision-making and offer a spiritual lead for the couple, we might have expected Ananias' decision to cheat God and then lie to Peter to have automatically impacted both himself and his wife. Significantly, however, Peter holds Ananias and then Sapphira independently to account and demands that they each personally decide their own fate. Ananias' actions are not taken as representative of Sapphira; he is not considered to have acted as "the priest" in his home, but rather as an individual and equal

---

[8] Gordon Fee, *"The Cultural Context of Ephesians 5:18-6:9,"* Priscilla Papers (Winter 2002), 4

member of a marriage partnership. As such, his wife was called to account in her own right and, by her own actions, implicated herself and bore the punishment in her own right.

It seems then from Scripture that the new covenant in Christ instituted a new equality for men and women, even stretching to reform the socially constructed relationship of husband and wife and create level ground at the foot of the cross where men and women, married or not, are equal in Christ.

How then is Paul's use of "head" to be understood?

## Understanding the pattern of head and shoulders government

There are several suggestions by scholars discussing the meaning of headship from the Greek (see also above). What is clear is that headship does not convey the same sense of ultimate authority that our English translation automatically assumes. The picture is not that of a general commanding his troops, but rather of a body in which each member has to play its part for the whole to function well[9].

One picture which may be helpful is that of the pattern of head and shoulders government in the Bible. Within the Godhead, the Father is the head – source of life and being – while the government rests on Jesus' shoulders (Isaiah 6:9). In the Kingdom, Jesus is the head of the Church (source of its life and being), while the Ephesians 4

---

[9] I Believe in Male Headship *by Gilbert Bilezikian* http://www.cbeinternational.org/?q=content/i-believe-male-headship

ministries and offices of apostles, prophets, pastors, teachers and evangelists are its government. In local church structure, the senior leader is the head with the elders as the shoulders. On that pattern, in the family the husband is the head with the wife as the shoulders. Only together does the body in each of these cases function correctly – head and shoulders need to operate in harmony with each other. The sense is of complementarity, as instituted in the Garden of Eden, rather than rulership and hierarchy which were the result of the Fall.

## The mix of marriage and ministry

There has been a conflict for married couples who are also involved in ministry. While the traditional stereotype of the pastor and pastor's wife still endures in some circles, mostly the conflict is over what authority a woman has in her own right in ministry if her husband is also in ministry. More complicated still is when the wife has a ministry call in the church but her husband does not. If the husband must always be her "head", how can she function in her ministry in church if his sphere of leadership is in business, for example?

Here we need to be clear that spiritual ministry and the anointing for leadership is never gender specific in Scripture. Paul's list of spiritual gifts in Romans 12, which includes leadership, does not differentiate on the basis of male or female. Nowhere does Paul make a distinction on the basis of gender and yet many conservative scholars will happily allow a woman with a gift of administration, service or hospitality to function freely without the need for headship/covering from her husband, yet would not feel as comfortable with a woman leader functioning as such in her own right. Yet, as we have seen earlier in our discussion, for example in the case of Deborah, God's choice was based on the best person for the job, not whether that person was male or female. In Deborah's case, her husband, Lappidoth, is clearly not in spiritual leadership but this does not disqualify Deborah.

Pastorally, some have argued that further conflict arises because a woman must juggle her roles as mother, wife and minister. Yet we have all also appreciated the need for fathers in the home too and know just how vital it is for a man to balance the roles of father, husband and minister. So while the model of husband and wife teams ministering together is admirable, there are enough exceptions in the Bible to force us to be cautious of presenting this as "the" model or rule for women who want to be in ministry, backing this up with a misunderstanding of Paul's use of the word "head".

## What about single women in ministry?

Many single and some married women followed Jesus (Luke 8:1-3). There were also many single and some married women in Paul's apostolic team. In Romans 16:3-16 there are 36 people who are named as being in Paul's team: 11 of these are women. One third of Paul's team were women and he was an unmarried man. Paul calls these women by various names: fellow soldiers, fellow workers, and fellow prisoners. Some even went to jail with him. These were powerful ministers in their own right.

In 1 Corinthians 7:34-35 Paul advocates celibacy as a gift given to certain people so that they can serve the Lord without the distraction of marriage responsibilities. This is advocated for women as well as for men. As Christ is the "head" of the single woman surely there is no need for the additional "covering" of a man. If she is called by God, then she should feel free to minister. The blessing and freedom of celibacy should be true for men and women equally. They can live a life devoted to God and serve Him.

In the history of the church the majority of pioneer missionaries have been women such as Jackie Pullinger and Amy Carmichael. If we had a hall of fame for the missionary activity of the last 200 years then you would find 75% would be women. The same is true in many social arenas.

# 7 Mothers and Fathers partnering for the nation

## *Back to the BIG picture!*

We have studied the difficult passages, looked at the Greek, and tried to understand the different theological view points about women in leadership. But before we get too overwhelmed by the micro-detail of all the arguments, it is vital that we do not lose sight of the more important things! Unfortunately, when we begin to debate some of these controversial issues, it stirs strong emotions and we can allow our words and actions to become very aggressive, and even destructive. We must remember that, even if we do differ from each other on our interpretation of these scriptures, we are called to love one another, to be kind to one another and respect one another. We are called to act with grace and love towards all people, both male and female, and we never have the right to be rude and angry with each other. Once, during the coffee break of a conference, a woman came to me and unleashed her bitterness about men and their attitudes to women. It was so full of hatred that I was shocked, especially when she later stood to lead the worship! However we feel we are treated as women in our respective churches we must remember it never gives us the right to become bitter or angry. We must forgive and move on even if there has been injustice. Some of my worst and most hurtful moments in church as a woman leader have been when a strong campaigner for the appropriate role of women in the church has targeted me. It can be a man or a woman – I have experienced both – but when they decide they need to correct your theology and then lay into you there is usually little grace or love but plenty of humiliation and sarcasm which can be so destructive and unloving. We need to be careful about using words to label people we do not agree with. Above all else let us agree to love one another whatever our theological differences concerning the role of women – please!

As we hear the prophetic voices calling women to take their place, some react to these words wondering if this battle is really a priority for our church today. Surely with church numbers declining in the West and many young people seeing Christianity as irrelevant, we have more important issues than "the role of women in the church" to consider, they argue. But as society becomes more dysfunctional and people become more lonely, the house of God has to become a place of hope. Most people who are coming to church and exploring their faith in this season have already experienced poor relationships in their family and are looking for role models in parenting and marriage that they can follow. They long to find a secure place with normal relationships where they can feel safe and flourish.

However, often they come into the church and discover that the same gender dysfunctionality they experienced at home is also present in the church. They find that men and women still have these issues in the church and their spiritual mothers and fathers are fighting too! For the sake of the lost we must sort this issue out. There are so many homes in our neighbourhoods that have dysfunctional models of parenting; people need to come into God's house and find a functioning family that models fathering and mothering well. It is time for the church to demonstrate the role of mothers and fathers in the nation.

## Power is released when love stands!

In this hour God is looking for men and women who will reverse the trends of negativity and hopelessness in our society. He is asking us to show people a better way. He is asking for mothers and fathers to arise in the land. We need to learn to work together in the house of God just as parents learn to do within their home. One of the gifts of good parenting is to create an atmosphere of love and acceptance where people can flourish.

All around us the cry of community is – "Does anyone care for me? Do I have any significance in someone's life? Does anyone value or notice what I do or who I am?" Just as in the home it is the role of the parents together to make each child feel special and honoured and give them a sense of purpose, so we need this sound in our communities. We need the father and mother heart that will create an environment of unconditional acceptance for those who are abandoned even if they feel worthless and have made poor life choices. One should never underestimate the power of determined love! When love stands up in a home, community or city, great power for change is released. We need the gift of spiritual mothers and fathers leading the way in our cities and streets once again.

## Mothers and Fathers in the land

Unfortunately, the idea of mothers and fathers standing up and taking their place of influence in our society can be a picture of hell for some. Our reaction to this image is so heavily influenced by our personal experience. If we have had a poor role model of a dad or mum in our home, our reaction can be very negative. However, true motherhood is a gift to our community and families. So we need to find grace to forgive and then have courage to look at the characteristics of good mothering and rebuild the broken places of our heart. Across the nation, research shows that there is a huge lack of secure parenting being modeled in our homes, so now more than ever the church needs to take the challenge and demonstrate how to be true fathers and mothers in the community. As we consider fathers and mothers partnering together in cooperation, let us read this scripture in Genesis:

**Genesis 1:27**

*So God created man in his own image, in the image of God he created him; male and female he created them.*

Here we read that God creates "man" as male and female, not as one solitary individual who personifies the fullness of God, but as two people who together represent the "oneness" of the image of God. So we need to understand that as we work "shoulder to shoulder" as the two genders in the ministry, we reflect more completely the image of God to others. There are characteristics of God which we carry in our female distinctiveness that, when working together with the male characteristics, will complement and more fully complete the picture of His image. We need each other!

There have been many debates and books written about the role of women in the church and their appropriate position in leadership. But rather than getting stuck on our definitions of what is leadership and the appropriate roles for women, I feel we should look at the model of a home. In a good working model of parenting, the husband and wife respect each other's gifts and allow each to function in their area of strength for the blessing of the home. In the early days of parenting the mother often appears to assume a strong leadership role, giving most of the instructions and leading the family through the time of change with the arrival of the baby. She often organizes the routines, gives endless instructions and practical advice to the new father who supports her as a new mother. As the family finds its new rhythm the father then finds his place and throughout the life of the home there is an ebb and flow of leadership and cooperation as the father and mother raise their children. I believe that we need to find this place of cooperation between the genders in the church too so that we work together for the good of the community.

## *We need mothers too!*

Over ten years ago now I was attending a church planting conference in Norway. As I entered the hall I quickly realized I was one of the few women present and the only female speaker. The first session started and the speaker spoke about the need for good fathers in your life. He shared powerfully about finding a mentor and friend to help you in the ministry as you begin to plant your church. Using the illustration of Paul and Timothy he then challenged these young church planters to consider whether they needed a father in their life. At the end of this moving session he called people forward if they wanted prayer because they had not had a father figure in their lives. I remember sitting and being amazed as 85% of these young people went forward. This was a precious "father and sons" moment so I sat and watched and prayed.

But then something happened which changed my life. In the midst of the altar prayer time I recognized many young men that I knew so I began to pray for them as I sat in my seat. Many of them were sobbing and I felt their distress as they processed their lack of a father. I longed for someone to go and comfort them, touch them and even hug them. But the men who were praying just quickly touched their foreheads and moved on, leaving them alone. The sound of the crying increased and I felt a longing to go to them but sat still knowing this was a time for the "fathers" to minister, not a woman. Then, suddenly, in the midst of this sobbing one young man that I knew began to crawl towards me to where I was sitting on the front row. Once he arrived in front of me he thrust his head into my lap and began to weep loudly and say something again and again. Through his tears I could not hear what he was saying at first but then I understood. He was exclaiming: "BUT we need MOTHERS too...we need mothers too!!"

As these words resonated in my heart, they changed my life. I heard the cry of a generation saying they need to have a mother figure in their life. I realized that emotionally healthy young people benefit from the influence of both a mum and a dad in their world at home and the same is true in church. Since that time I have asked God for ways to help the next generation of leaders know the heart of fathers and mothers on their journey to maturity. They want both male and female role models in their lives.

## Is there a Mother in the House?

"Where is Mum? I need help!" The urgent cry rang through the house as my son expressed his frustration at not being able to find his keys and now he was running late. When I appeared I was greeted with a look of relief and we duly found the keys and his day was back on track. This type of scenario plays itself out in homes all across the world. Mums are a necessary glue to keep life and relationships working smoothly in our homes. We all appreciate the need for a mother in our homes and few would dispute this, but somehow we have lost the power of understanding the gift and necessity of the mother heart in our community and church life.

## Let the mothers arise!

In Judges we read of a woman called Deborah who became a mother figure in her nation and community.

**Judges 5:7**
*Village life in Israel ceased, ceased until I, Deborah, **arose,
arose a mother in Israel.***

Here Deborah identifies that the community function and relationship, that is village life, is breaking down. But rather than asking who is going to stop the trend she decides to stand up and act. She arises with her mother heart and begins to influence her community with the grace of a mother in her nation. We often talk about the leadership vacuum, the lack of fatherhood and male role models and the terrible statistics resulting from marriage and family breakdown. We have looked for a man but maybe the community transformation we seek will require men and women working together. Just as we need our mums to help us in the home, so we need the mother hearted leaders back in our communities and nations!

Again and again history teaches us that women have played a vital role in shaping nations and helping communities in times of trouble, war and change. Women have helped pioneer movements which have influenced the laws on voting rights for women, freedom for slaves, kindness to animals and justice for the poor. The cry of the mother heart has influenced our world view and made us more compassionate and caring in our legislation. I believe that we are in a time of shaking and change once again and God is asking the church to arise in this hour. But we need to consider how we are going to release our women to work alongside our fatherhood figures to bring back a greater influence of God into our culture. Just as a good home needs both the voice of a mum and a dad, so I believe healthy communities need both the expression of mothers and of fathers in the land if we are to hit the mark. Sometimes God waits for us to get correctly positioned in our working relationships before the community and the nation receives its blessing! In Deborah's day, village or community life was declining until a woman stood up and reversed the trend. Will we recognize the mothers in the land in these days and allow them to arise?

## Some leaders are born women

As I opened an interestingly shaped letter, a fridge magnet fell out of the packing and the words made me smile: "Some leaders are born women!" it confidently declared. I then opened the card and was surprised to see that this gift had been sent by a man who had recently attended a seminar that I had led. He wrote in the card that he had been blessed to watch me lead a day of prayer in his city with confident authority but an unashamedly feminine style. He concluded his card by saying he had found it a healing occasion as the female role models in his life had been unhelpful and often in the church he had noticed that women either led like men, hiding their feminine side, or did not lead at all despite their gifting. This made me think about the need for women to model a healthy leadership pattern that does not deny their femininity. I believe that in these days we are seeing many significant young women answer the call to leadership in the church and community and they are looking for mentors and role models. Often their only reference and advice for the roles they desire to fill come from men and so their leadership styles can become confused. We need older women to model healthy leadership styles for our next generation so that they can know how to lead effectively. We need to train our women to lead with authority, as daughters of the King, without apology for being female but also without any defensive aggression rooted in feminism. Young men too want to see this healthy male and female leadership modeled as they begin to learn how they can work together in their marriages and families. Deborah was a judge and a leader who worked closely with the male national leaders. She modeled this effectively in a culture that did not usually have female national leadership; her example still challenges us to arise and lead today.

# 8 The Cry for Spiritual Motherhood

This type of spiritual motherhood has nothing to do with age, experience, or even gender, but is part of the expression of God's character. You do not have to be a natural mum to exhibit the qualities of spiritual motherhood. Our spiritual authority is greater than our natural experience and position but the natural expression does give us the illustration of the spiritual principle. So when we look at a good role model of a natural mother we can gain insight into this gift of spiritual mothering.

So what is a mother? There are numerous funny quotes but the following is a more serious attempt to define the mother's role:

A MOTHER is one who is there – to nurture, nourish, nurse, care for, look after, protect, shelter, watch over, take care of, pamper. They baby, spoil, indulge, fuss over, overprotect. Mothers bring forth, deliver, bear, carry, and birth.

Tenderness, kindness, compassion, birthing, patience and long-suffering are amongst the characteristics that we identify with the mother image and of course we can all think of a hundred other qualities and definitions too! But let us look at some of these qualities in light of their spiritual nature.

## Boys can be mothers too!

This cry of spiritual motherhood can be expressed by men too! The natural example of motherhood is demonstrated by women birthing and caring for their children but the spiritual manifestation of motherhood is not a "girls only" activity. The natural illustration is usually defined by our roles and gender but the spiritual demonstration is broader. In the following passages we see two single men describe their spiritual passion in motherhood and birthing terms. Firstly, Jesus speaks of his breaking heart for Jerusalem:

**Matthew 23:37**
37 *Jerusalem, Jerusalem, you who kill the prophets and stone those sent to you, how often I have longed to gather your children together, as a (mother) hen gathers her chicks under her wings, and you were not willing.*

Then we also read of the apostle Paul, considered a hardened "man's man" and anti-women by some, also speak with a soft, caring heart for the church. This would be considered more emotional and "girls speak" by most. He is not showing the fatherhood face here but his incredible spiritual capacity as a mother who loves the church.

**2 Corinthians 2:3-5**
*I wrote as I did, so that when I came I would not be distressed by those who should have made me rejoice. I had*

*confidence in all of you, that you would all share my joy. 4
For I wrote to you out of great distress and anguish of heart
and with many tears, not to grieve you but to let you know
the depth of my love for you.*

**Galatians 4:19-20**
*My dear children, for whom I am again in the pains of
childbirth until Christ is formed in you, 20 how I wish I could
be with you now and change my tone, because I am
perplexed about you!*

So whether male or female, God wants to stir the cry of
spiritual motherhood again in the church. He is calling
men to stand alongside women and birth a new day for
the church. Let us read the cry of the prophet Jeremiah:

**Jeremiah 30:6-7**
*Ask and see: Can a man bear children?  Then why do I see
every strong man with his hands on his stomach like a
woman in labor, every face turned deathly pale? 7 How awful
that day will be!  No other will be like it.  It will be a time of
trouble for Jacob, but he will be saved out of it.*

Here Jeremiah describes a shift in the spiritual
atmosphere when he observes men becoming birthers in
a time of trouble in the nation. This prophet is watching a
rising generation of men birthing a day of rescue in the
midst of national pain and difficulty. This call is beyond
our natural gender: it stirs us to the core of our spirit.

## Mothers are Birthers

In the natural realm it is the women who give birth and
most men I know are very happy about that! However, in
other spheres of life many women would love to take
some initiative and birth a new project but this can be
viewed by the church as inappropriate leadership. But

we need to understand that in the heart of a woman there is a birther – she loves to watch dreams and projects come forth. Often she may not want to take full responsibility for the resulting "baby" and will need help, advice and financial support, but she does long to birth a project.

## Mother of Life

**Genesis 3:20**
*Adam named his wife* **Eve, because she would become the mother of all the living.**

We are all aware that if there is life there will be growth. Mothers are used to handling the different seasons of life and the changes brought through growth. As mums we understand the cost of mothering the living! We experience this cost whenever we trek to the shoe store to replace a fairly new pair of shoes that are already too small for our child's rapidly growing feet! We are made to be in the midst of rapid growth and life. That is when mums do best!

## Mother of Nations

**Genesis 17:16**
*I will bless her and will surely give you a son by her.* **I will bless her so that she will be the mother of nations; kings of peoples will come from her.**

When God promises Abraham that he will become a father of many nations He also specifically speaks about Sarah, Abraham's wife, declaring that she would also be a mother of nations. I believe here we see that this promise of God for the generations could only be fulfilled if both Abraham and Sarah took their place together. We all acknowledge that in the natural world we need a man and a woman to come together before they can be fruitful and birth the next generation but somehow, in the church, we have only emphasized the role of fathers and not of mothers. Maybe we would have greater fruitfulness if we discovered how we can work effectively together as mums and dads in the house of God.

I believe that in our church lives we need to understand how we can work together as leaders with the projects and visions God has given many women for our communities and nations and, by pooling our experience and expertise, help them birth the dreams of heaven.

## The best mum in the world

As mums there is nothing more satisfying than receiving a letter or mother's day card written by one of your nearly adult kids expressing their gratitude for your time and love. It makes the memory of every hard day worth it. We all want to be the best mum in the world! So how can we train and prepare ourselves to be the best mums in our communities and world? What do we need to develop in our lives?

I have learnt that, before we can be effective mothers, we need to know that we are significant daughters. We need to go on a journey with God where we allow Him to show us how much He loves us. We need to have deep heart surgery so that the brokenness that we have experienced in our lives can be healed first. We need to be secure children before we can be mature parents. As we begin to desire to be used as parents to our communities we find God challenges every area of our lives, revealing the foundations that are rooted in insecurity and then bringing healing. Then we are ready to go and be mothers and fathers in the land.

## Creating right atmospheres for healthy living

As we step into our broken communities with God's heart we need to create the caring atmospheres that will birth fresh hope and tenderness into the lives around us. Inside every human being is the basic need to know that they are unique and special. So let us look at some of the mindsets we need to confront and the Kingdom values of God we need to release by our words and actions.

## Significance – revealing we are of great value and self-worth

It is our privilege to be God's communicators of this message. We read the following in this passage in Isaiah:

### Isaiah 43:4
*Since you are precious and honoured in my sight, and because I love you, I will give men in exchange for you, and people in exchange for your life.*

As mothers in the community we need to fortify the confidence of each individual, and strengthen their belief that they are of value to God. Just as a mother in her own home will speak encouragement and hope into the child who feels a failure and unable to attempt the task in hand, so we need to find the hopeless and speak life into their crushed identities. We need to come in the opposite spirit to the atmosphere of negativity and failure that shrouds so many people's lives and release the sound of value, success and honour. Mothers are great cheer leaders and we need to champion the broken and marginalized. As mothers, let us use our words and actions to underline the value and significance of each life.

## Destiny – confirming that I am made for purpose

In the following scriptures we read of the heart of God towards us:

### Isaiah 43:1

*But now, this is what the LORD says-- he who created you, O Jacob, he who formed you, O Israel: "Fear not, for I have redeemed you; I have summoned you by name; you are mine."*

### Jeremiah 29:11

*"For I know the plans I have for you," declares the LORD, "plans to prosper you and not to harm you, plans to give you hope and a future."*

God created us and also planned a future for us. He made plans for our lives and these are the best plans possible. As we arise to be mothers in the land we need to endorse this sense of destiny in each person. They need to know they have a purpose in life. With the increase of suicide in young adults and the numbers of youth on anti-depressants and suffering from stress-related illness, we need to release this sound of hope. So many have been born without this sense of purpose and they feel they are just a nuisance. But we are not a nuisance to God. In Song of Songs chapter 7:10 we read: *"I belong to my lover, and his desire is for me."* We need to show those around us that God desires us and wants to be with us. He gave His life for us and we are partners with Him for purpose. He has work for us to do which will bring great satisfaction. So, as women, we need to encourage the work force and show them their God-given tasks.

## Security – now I can trust again

Here we read in the Psalms:

**Psalm 9:10**
*Those who know your name will trust in you, for you, LORD, have never forsaken those who seek you.*

For many the risk of learning to trust again is huge. But the tender persuasion of a mother is amazing. I was in the park recently with my granddaughter. While she was playing I found myself watching two parents trying to persuade their toddler down a steep slide. The dad tried to push his two-year-old down but he would not let go and, as a struggle ensued, became more adamant that he would not do it. Eventually the father gave up as the child began to scream. But now the mum climbed the slide and sat down next to the boy and slowly began to win his trust. After many patient conversations, he eventually released his tight grip on the rails and slid down a few metres where his mum caught him. Each time he climbed to the top she increased the distance of her catching position by a few metres, winning his trust, until eventually the boy let go and slid the whole distance. Then the dad swapped with the mum, ready to catch his son now that his confidence seemed to be restored but the boy cried – "No, daddy, I do not trust you!" However, by the end of play, both mum and dad were chasing their son who was throwing himself down the slide with no trace of fear! Here I watched the patient kindness of a mother restoring trust in her son when he was overcome with fear.

All through our society we see the shipwrecked lives of those who have lost their ability to trust. They believed in marriage once but were then abandoned. They loved their father but then suffered abuse. They enjoyed work but were then sacked. There are so many different circumstances of loss that all leave our trust capacity depleted. We need the sound of the patient mother heart that will come and sit alongside the fearful and help them find their confidence again. Sometimes we need the shouted command and instruction but often, when we are fearful, we need the patient sound of reassurance and a helping hand. So let us release this sound into the lives of the hurting around us. .

## Forgiveness – help me, I am in a mess

I do not know what the state of play was like in your home but I know in our house, especially when my brothers had made a mistake, they would ask if Mum was there! If the school report was bad, or you had just bashed the car, or spilt paint on the carpet, you called for mum so that you could negotiate your pardon with her first. Somehow, mums have this reputation for being the "soft touch".

I believe that it is true in the church too. When someone

knows they have made a poor life choice and they need help, they often look for the mother figure to help them. Just as in the home situation, when a child wakes up and vomits everywhere, the cry goes out "Mummy, I have made a mess – Mum, please help me!" When there is a mess we usually call for our mums to come and clear it up. In the same way we need to be ready to release our women to go and pastorally help the sons and daughters "clean up their mess" so that they can know that they are forgiven and be ready to live lives free from their mess. We need to be ready as fathers and mothers to help those who want to be free to get clean. It takes great courage for someone to expose their mess and we need to be ready to help them clean it up. Mums, we need to be on cleaning duty!

## Servanthood – ready to sacrifice for others' wellbeing

This is the time to train the heart of the servant. Nothing challenges your selfishness like becoming a mother. For me, the hardest thing was sacrificing my bed and sleep in those early years of motherhood. In Matthew we read this scripture:

**Matthew 20:26**

*Not so with you. Instead, whoever wants to become great among you must be your servant, and whoever wants to be first must be your slave--just as the Son of Man did not come to be served, but to serve, and to give his life as a ransom for many.*

As mothers we need to model this heart of a servant and so undermine the sound of selfishness in our culture. The heart of the servant desires to make others look good. It is not easily threatened by others' success. We can serve others and let them succeed beyond us. Just as a mother feels great pride when her children do well in school or sports days so we will feel good when we watch those around us do well.

## Generosity – knowing I have something to give

Often as a mother you can feel that your needs come last. But the life of mothering teaches you to give and sacrifice. As mothers you find yourself giving generously of your time and money just so that you can watch others mature and grow into their destiny. We need to learn the art of being generous givers. This is the heart of motherhood. Our God is a God of great generosity and we too need to learn to become givers and investors. Often we will not see the fruit of our investment in people's lives immediately and, if we are not careful, we can become resentful and feel that people take from us. But, just as in the natural, if you wait you will see the growth of your children into all you expected and they will bring you great delight. So will you go and give generously to those around you? The Bible gives us these standards for our lives in the following scriptures:

**Psalm 37:26**
*The righteous are always generous and lend freely; their children will be blessed.*

**1 Timothy 6:18**

*Command them to do good, to be rich in good deeds, and to be generous and willing to share.*

So, in this season, let God examine your heart and evaluate it. He is preparing the heart of the church to be mothers and fathers in this generation for the sake of the nation. The testing of our heart is never pleasant, but once we have passed the test, we will reap an incredible harvest in the lives around us. The church and society are watching for those who will love them when they are ugly, those who will show them unconditional love when they get it wrong, and those who will still love them when they are in a mess. We must be ready to arise as fathers and mothers in the nation and ask God to show us how we can "parent" the community once again.

# 9 Selah – Pause, stop, think & reflect!

It was Speech Day at Nicola's school when the end of year awards and prizes would be announced. A sense of expectation filled the auditorium as the headmaster of this Christian school took his place at the microphone and began to announce the winners. "Nicola Hickson is awarded the prize for outstanding leadership," he announced, and my parental heart swelled with pride: she was 10 years old. But, as I watched Nicola approach the stage to collect her certificate, I knew something was wrong. She did not walk forward with her head up and smiling – she was scowling and her head was bowed. I was confused. Finally the speeches ended and I waited in the car for the children to arrive for their lift home. Nicola appeared and before I could congratulate or hug her she opened the car door, jumped in and burst into tears. She then proceeded to tear up the newly acquired certificate into tiny pieces. I waited for her to speak and finally she exclaimed: "Mum, it is not fair, they just humiliated me. I am a girl and they just called me "bossy" in front of the whole school!" I ached inside as, already at this young age, Nicola was discerning that some people do not see leadership as a positive attribute in a girl!

## Pause - now consider some pastoral issues

So let us reflect for a moment on how our language and behaviour concerning the role of women communicates to people around us. Over the years Gordon and I have handled many pastoral situations where precious people have been devastated by harsh treatment because of these issues. Even as we conclude this book, my main cry is this: PLEASE let us love one another and no hate mail! Good people do get damaged.

I remember the occasion when a newly married couple sat in our lounge in tears. They had just returned from honeymoon to find a letter that had rocked their world. Sally (not her real name) had a radical encounter with Jesus at 17 years old and then returned to school and started a revival in her sixth form college. Over the next two years she had 70 to 80 young people meeting together weekly at school. She then approached her church and started a Friday night chat and youth night. This grew, and by the time she left for university this church, which previously had only a few young people, now had a thriving youth and young professionals group led by Sally and her team. Even while at university Sally would meet with the home team at the beginning of each term and help with the programme and lead. During this time a young man, John (not his real name either!), was saved and fell in love with Sally; now they were married and back from honeymoon. But this letter had shocked them: "Dear Sally and John, we want to congratulate you on your recent marriage but need to point out to you that it would no longer be appropriate for you, Sally, to lead the youth work as a woman and so we have asked Peter (a false name again) to take this role. John, you would of course be welcome to come to the leadership meetings…etc". When this couple chatted to Peter he was, in his own words, "gutted" and did not want the role without Sally being around! All around there was anger, tears and pain! There must be a better way to handle these situations!

I remember another occasion when a man warmly greeted me at a conference and expressed his appreciation for me. He then said: "Rachel, I will not of course be coming to your seminar as I do not believe that I should place myself under a woman's authority but I have ordered the CD and will enjoy listening to you later!".

On another occasion I was speaking with a precious woman, now a widow, who serves the children in her church. For years she has headed up the Sunday school, local schools work and youth programme. She is an amazing communicator and the children LOVE her. She was expressing some of her pain at being excluded from the leaders' discussion when they seek God for the themes and curriculum for the following year. The pastor appreciates and respects her highly but, since her husband died, she has not been able to attend any of the leaders' functions, whether the social meal at Christmas or the planning meetings. This church has a policy of no women on the leadership team. However, in reality this woman does lead all the children's work and after these leadership evenings the pastor always makes an appointment to come and see her to discuss the children's work and ask for her input. Before her husband died she was able to attend with him, although he never taught or was involved in any of the children's programmes. But this isolation from the team at a time of loss was so hard for her to handle. Through her tears she expressed what was in her heart: "But I haven't changed, I am still the same person, so why am I now considered a 'dangerous' person because I am single and widowed?" Surely, as the church, we must be able to find a kinder way to handle these situations. So let us STOP, reflect and think about the impact of some of our actions on people we are called to love.

## Stop thinking for a moment – it is time to pray

We have studied the difficult passages and challenged our mindsets. We have looked at the stories of women in the Bible and learnt from their example. We have considered our views on leadership and discussed the role of women in the church. But now it is time to stop thinking and start praying! Why not just take a moment and ask God if He has anything He wants to say to you? Take a moment to reflect and pray. Ask God to reveal to you what you need to change, if anything, and who you need to forgive, if anyone! Take a moment to surrender your life to God afresh. Remove every wrong limitation you have placed upon yourself or others. In this moment dedicate your life anew for the purposes of God. Declare over your life that nothing is going to hold you back – you are free!

So, let us pray…

*Father, right now I ask for your Spirit of revelation and peace to come upon each person as we stop and pray. We ask you to take our minds, take our ways of thinking and our attitudes, and reveal to us your heart. Right now we pray that you will clarify for us any confusion and you will enable us to forgive any offenses or pain we have carried. Come, Holy Spirit, and heal your church. We desire to reflect your beauty in our lives. Thank you for your peace and wisdom. Amen.*

## Release my frozen assets

I can hear the cry – "Release my frozen assets!" ringing clearly across the nations. Although this is not an easy journey to navigate I believe it is an essential one for the church to face. Will we let our women go to be the messengers of Jesus in their communities?

Recently, I was standing in the lounge of my married daughter, Nicola Douglass, in Melbourne Australia. I was beginning to prepare my heart for the long journey home and leaving my precious girl and grandchildren in another nation. But I know I cannot complain, for I have only myself to blame. I raised this champion princess with an expectation that God would use her to have a powerful impact to influence her world. In this season, I can see the precious rose I tended while young now blossoming into an effective communicator and leader. As Tim and Nicola begin to pioneer the new Melbourne Hillsong church I know God will use her alongside Tim to have an impact. It is time to release her once again to go to the nations. As I am standing considering these things, a little hand suddenly clasps mine. I look down to see my granddaughter, Leila, holding my hand. "Nanny, hurry", she cries, as she pulls me to the door. "YES", she screams as we run to the garage, "we are going to church and I am going to sing!". As she jumps into the car I realize: here is another leader in the making. Here is another delicate rose that will grow and then take her part in God's story in the nations.

So let us arise and go forward as men and women who love and respect one another and work together for His glory. It is time to reverse the curse of the gender war and work together for the sake of the harvest!

# Appendix

*Detailed analysis of 1 Timothy 2:11-12*

### Didasko

- *didaskein*, the verb "to teach" is not used to refer to the neutral activity of teaching, but to what is being taught. Tucker and Liefeld suggest that the word used by Paul for "teach" (*didasko*) has the formal sense of teaching doctrine, carrying the authoritative teachings of Jesus and the apostles to the new churches, rather than merely instructing converts, which neither Jews nor pagans would have accepted from a woman. Teaching is defined "in terms of the truth which it bears (1Timothy 4:2; Titus 1:9)", and teachers by the truth or error of their message (1Timothy 1:7, 2:7; 2 Timothy 1:11, 4:3-4; Titus 2:3).

- Paul's focus then, is that women in Ephesus should learn, rather than teach, doctrine and he explains why in verses 13 and 14, using Genesis 2 and 3 figuratively to illustrate his point. Paul's logic is to prohibit women from teaching, not because they should be subject to male authority, but because a deceived woman was the problem at the Fall and is a similar danger to the early church.

- Eve illustrates the urgent need for women in Ephesus to learn because the danger of a deceived woman was the problem in Eden. It is because the serpent approached Eve (as false teachers are preying on women) that Paul argues

115

that women in Ephesus need to be taught. Adam's prior creation (v.13) explains why it was Eve, not Adam, who was deceived, Adam as a "type" representing in his prior creation male social advantage within patriarchal society. As Eve's deception illustrates the current situation of deceived, ill-educated women in Ephesus, so Adam's priority illustrates the contemporary culture of predominantly male teachers. Paul's reminder that Adam was created first perhaps also had the intention of countering Gnostic claims of female precedence.

- Contrary to the view prevalent in Jewish and Hellenistic literature that women were inherently more gullible and prone to deception than men, Paul stresses that the woman "became a sinner" through deception – it was not part of her nature (verse 14). Elsewhere in this letter, Paul names two male false teachers (1Timothy 1:20), aware that men too are capable of being deceived, also using Eve figuratively to stand for deception of both men and women (2 Corinthians 11:3).

- Whilst Paul stresses that Eve's disobedience involved deception whereas Adam's did not (1Timothy 2:14), he does not exonerate Adam from sin, using him figuratively to represent the sin of humanity (1Corinthians 15:22; Romans 5:12-18).

- The call to learn in quietness and submission (2:11) has traditionally been interpreted as reinforcing a principle of female subordination. However, the grammar of the text indicates that it is not to male authority that women are to submit, but to the teaching of the church (see Perriman). Submission does not take a personal object but describes a willingness to be taught, contrasting with the kind of domineering teaching that Paul addresses in verse 12.

## Authentein

- Considerable scholarly debate about this unusual word, which appears only here in the New Testament, suggests that the traditional translation "have authority over" is extremely unlikely. If the ordinary exercise of authority is what Paul has in mind, he could have used "exousia", as he does elsewhere in the New Testament (e.g. 1 Corinthians 7:4, 11:10). This suggests that he had a different meaning in mind.

- Bearing in mind the possible Gnostic content of the heretical teaching, the Kroegers suggest that Paul uses "authentein" with the sense of "the ultimate creative source" or "origin of". The verse would then be translated "I do not allow a woman to teach nor to proclaim herself author of man."

- C. Kroeger argues that "authenteō" has a range of meanings: "to begin something, to be primarily responsible for a condition or action (especially murder); to rule, to dominate; to usurp power or rights from another; to claim ownership, sovereignty or authorship". Kroeger, C. (1986) 1 Timothy 2:12, A Classicist's View. In A. Mickelsen (Ed.), Women, Authority & the Bible. (pp. 225-243). Downer's Grove, IL: Intervarsity Press.

- Others have argued that a more usual sense of the word is "to domineer", "to usurp authority", "to assume a stance of independent authority, give orders to, dictate to."

- Perriman argues that the word focuses on the use, rather than the possession of authority. The exercise of "*authenteō*" means the object of the verb "*does something* as a result." Perriman therefore sees Paul's choice of word as relating specifically to what Eve did to Adam, exerting negative influence over him, which resulted in his sin. Paul therefore commands women to learn and not teach or induce men to accept false teaching as Eve did. Paul's choice of this word addresses a specific abuse of power, or way of exercising authority, rather than forbidding women to hold positions of authority per se.

In light of the false teaching, having argued that women should learn, Paul affirms marriage (1Timothy 4:3) and child-rearing as part of God's plan of salvation. 1 Timothy 5:14 then elaborates 2:15, Paul overtly stating that younger widows should marry and have children to prevent the spread of false teaching. Older women are to instruct younger ones (Titus 2:3-5) to love their husbands and children and to undertake the traditional domestic responsibilities of contemporary culture. This emphasis on maintaining domestic life (also directed at male leaders 1Timothy 3:4-5, 12; Titus 1:6) has a missionary focus, to preserve the reputation and witness of the church within wider society (1Timothy 3:7, 6:1; Titus 2:5).

# Bibliography & further reading:

- Ashley, Rosemary, "Not so with you", MPhil study, May 2005.

- Bailey, Dr Kenneth E. "Women in the New Testament: A Middle Eastern Cultural View", ANVIL Journal, 1994

- Bilezikain, Dr. Gilbert "Why Jesus Chose Male Apostles" in *Community 101: Reclaiming the local Church as Community of Oneness,* Zondervan, 1997.

- Bilezikian, Gilbert, *Beyond Sex Roles: what the Bible says about a woman's place in church and family,* Baker Academic, 3rd Revised Edition, 2006.

- Bilezikian, Gilbert, "I Believe in Male Headship", can be accessed at http://www.cbeinternational.org/?q=content/i-believe-male-headship

- Bushnell, Katharine C., *God's Word to Women,* Published via reprint, ed. Ray Munson, 1976.

- Christians for Biblical Equality website http://www.cbeinternational.org/?q=content/free-articles

- Cunningham, Loren and Hamilton, David Joel, *Why Not Women: A Biblical Study of Women in Missions, Ministry, and Leadership,* YWAM Publishing, 2000

- Epp, Eldon Jay *Junia: The First Woman Apostle,* Fortress Press 2005

- Fee, Gordon D., *The First Epistle to the Corinthians*, The New International Commentary on the NT, Eerdmans, 1987.

- Fee, Gordon D., "The Cultural Context of Ephesians 5:18-6:9," by Gordon D. Fee, can be accessed at http://www.cbeinternational.org/?q=content/cultural-context-ephesians-518-69

- God's Word to Women website http://godswordtowomen.org/scripture_study_articles.htm

- Grady, J. Lee, *10 Lies the Church Tells Women: How the Bible has been misused to keep women in spiritual bondage* – Creation House, 2001.

- Groothuis, Rebecca Merrill, *Good News for Women: a Biblical Picture of Gender Equality*, Baker Publishing Group, 1997.

- Groothuis, Rebecca Merrill, "The Bible and Gender Equality", can be accessed at http://www.cbeinternational.org/?q=content/bible-and-gender-equality

- Hull, Gretchen Gaebelein, *Equal to Serve: Women and Men Working Together Revealing the Gospel*, Baker Books, 2003

- Johnson, Alan, "A Christian Understanding of Submission: A Nonhierarchical- Complementarian Viewpoint", can be accessed at http://www.cbeinternational.org/?q=content/christian-understanding-submission-nonhierarchical-complementarian-viewpoint

- Kroeger, Richard Clark and Kroeger, Catherine Clark, *I Suffer Not a Woman: Rethinking I Timothy*

*2:11-15 in Light of Ancient Evidence*, Baker Academic, 1998.

- Perriman, Andrew, *Speaking of Women*, IVP, 1998.
- Pierce, Ronald W. and Groothuis, Rebecca Merrill, Editors, *Discovering Biblical Equality: Complementarity without Hierarchy*, Apollos, 2005.
- Piper, John and Grudem, Wayne, Editors, *Recovering Biblical Manhood and Womanhood: A Response to Evangelical Feminism*, Crossway, 2012.
- Scholer, David M., "The Evangelical Debate over Biblical 'Headship'" http://www.godswordtowomen.org/scholer.htm
- Scott, Martin and Birch, Peter, *For such a time as this*, P.S. promotions Ltd, 2001
- Silvoso, Ed, *Women: God's Secret Weapon*, Regal Books 2001
- Pierce, Chuck D., "Women arising now", chapter 9 in Pierce, Chuck D. and Wagner Systema, Rebecca, *The Future War of the Church*, Gospel Light Publications, 2001
- Vincent, Alan, "The whole truth about women", School of the Word, October 2006

# About the Authors – Rachel Hickson

Rachel Hickson is an internationally respected prayer leader and Bible teacher with a recognized prophetic gift. She teaches all over the world, and is in demand as a conference speaker.

At the age of 24 Rachel, with her husband, Gordon, worked alongside Reinhard Bonnke and the Christ for All Nations team in Africa. After just six weeks in Zimbabwe she almost lost her life in a horrific car accident, but was miraculously healed by God. This incident birthed in Rachel a desire to pray and to train others to realize the full potential of a praying church.

After returning from Africa in 1990, Rachel and her husband, Gordon, pastored a group of four churches in Hertfordshire and it was during this time that they established Heartcry Ministries with the call to train and equip people to be released into effective ministries. In 2005 Rachel and Gordon moved to Oxford where Gordon was the associate minister of St. Aldates Church for 6 years. In 2011 he moved to become the director of specialist missions and church planting projects, still based in Oxford.

Rachel travels internationally, visiting Europe, North America, Africa, India and Australia. Invitations come from a variety of denominational backgrounds, and both rural and city churches.

Rachel and Gordon have a passion to see cities transformed through the power of prayer and evangelism.

Rachel has been married to Gordon for over 30 years.

She is the mother of two married children, Nicola and David, and has two grandchildren, Leila and Cooper.

She is the author of 9 books:

*Supernatural Communication, the Privilege of Prayer*, and *Supernatural Breakthrough, The Heartcry for Change*, published by New Wine Ministries.

*Stepping Stones to Freedom, Pathway of Peace, Eat the Word Speak the Word and Run your Race* published by Monarch.

*Eat the Word Study Guide, Supernatural Communication Study Guide* and now *Release my frozen assets* published by Heartcry for Change.

# About the Authors – Helen Azer

Helen was born in England but grew up in Egypt where she lived for the first sixteen years of her life. She is half English and half Egyptian. Helen went to a German school in Cairo so from her early years developed a passion for other nations, cultures and languages. She returned to the UK with her family in 1994 to finish her schooling and went on to study History and German at Christ Church College, Oxford.

While in Germany studying the history of the Reformation, Helen felt God's call to full-time Christian ministry. She trained at Wycliffe Hall theological college, Oxford, and was ordained as a minister in the Church of England in 2004. She completed the practical side of her training on staff at St Aldates Church, Oxford, in 2007. Helen is now Associate Minister with Heartcry Ministries where she has worked for over five years and also volunteers her time at St Andrews Church in Cumnor, Oxford.

Helen enjoys the privilege of touching people's lives at home and abroad through preaching, teaching and training. She loves connecting with the bigger picture of what God is doing nationally and internationally as she travels with Heartcry and ministers in conferences, retreats and training days.

# Heartcry Ministries & Heartcry for Change Information

We work with churches and people from many nations and denominations to equip them in the following areas:

> ➤ PRAYER – Training an army of ordinary people in prayer schools and seminars to become confident to break the sound barrier and pray informed, intelligent and passionate prayers.

> ➤ PROPHETIC – Equipping the church to be an accurate prophetic voice in the nation by teaching in training schools and conferences the principles of the prophetic gift. We seek to train people who are passionate to know the presence of God, are available to hear His voice and then learn to speak His word with accuracy so that lives can be touched and changed.

> ➤ WOMEN – Delivering a message of hope to women across the nations and cultures to help them arise with a new confidence so that they can be equipped and ready to fulfil their destiny and execute their kingdom purpose.

> ➤ CAPITAL CITIES – Standing in the capital cities of the world, working with government institutions, businesses and the church and then crying out for a new alignment of the natural and spiritual government in these places. A cry for London and beyond.

> ➤ BUSINESS & FINANCE – Connecting business people with their kingdom purpose so that provision can partner more effectively with vision and accelerate the purpose of God in nations. Connecting commerce, community and church for change!